THE
BULLMASTIFF

Peerless Protector

GERALDINE M. ROACH AND JACK SHASTID

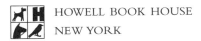
HOWELL BOOK HOUSE
NEW YORK

Howell Book House
A Simon & Schuster Macmillan Company
1633 Broadway
New York, NY 10019-6785

Macmillan Publishing books may be purchased for business or sales promotional use. For information please write: Special Markets Department, Macmillan Publishing USA, 1633 Broadway, New York, NY 10019-6785.

Library of Congress Cataloging-in-Publication

Roach, Geraldine.
    The bullmastiff : peerless protector / Geraldine Roach and Jack Shastid.
        p.   cm.
    ISBN 0-87605-081-X
    1. Bullmastiff.   I. Shastid, Jack.   II. Title.
SF429.B86R625   1998
636.73—dc21
                                                        98-12385
                                                        CIP

Manufactured in the United States of America

10 9 8 7 6 5 4 3 2

Cover and book design by George McKeon

Contents

A Note from the Authors

We have attempted in this book to inform the reader of the origins of the Bullmastiff, the reason for the breed's existence, its early years and the condition of the breed today. In the chapters on the care and husbandry of the Bullmastiff, we have attempted to inform our readers of the most modern techniques and knowledge available. We have also listed the people who helped form the Bullmastiff as we know it. We offer our sincere apologies if we have inadvertently missed the achievements of someone.

We hope you will enjoy this book. Our thanks and gratitude go to the American Kennel Club and the Kennel Club of the United Kingdom for the use of their libraries and records. Special thanks go to Harry and Beryl Colliass, Oldwell Bullmastiffs, for the many hours they have allowed us to spend at Horseshoe Lea reminiscing about the dogs they have known. We have made many new friends during the course of researching and writing this book. To them we say a very heartfelt thank you. Our gratitude also is due our Editor, Seymour Weiss, for being so gracious while the finishing touches were painstakingly being added.

CHAPTER 1

Is a Bullmastiff Right for You?

The Bullmastiff was originally developed to work with gamekeepers in Great Britain, protecting game reserves and discouraging poachers. Despite its utilitarian origins, it is now first and foremost a family dog. It is a breed that focuses on the human members of its household, much as the early dogs focused their attention on the gamekeeper. This characteristic makes the Bullmastiff ideally suited to the job of companion guard, rather than simply a property protector.

THE BULLMASTIFF AT HOME

A naturally clean breed, the Bullmastiff thrives in the home environment. In our opinion, it does not fare as well nor develop to its fullest potential as a yard or kennel dog.

The choice of male or female is a personal preference, but it is wise to remember that Bullmastiff males rarely get along together at maturity. The breed will tolerate cats, small pets and farm animals if they have been socialized to them as youngsters. However, do not expect an adult Bullmastiff that has never seen a chicken in its life to refrain from chasing one, with possible murderous intentions, should the opportunity arise.

The Bullmastiff is now first and foremost a family dog.

Bullmastiff pups should have some rudimentary training early on.

Bullmastiffs often tolerate other pets, if socialized with them early in life. This is Wesley with his bunny. (Geraldine Roach)

Puppies are free spirits, but that puppyhood exuberance will give way to a quieter demeanor as the puppy becomes an adult. The statement that the tree will grow as the twig is bent was never truer than as it applies to the Bullmastiff. Do not let the puppy do anything you would not wish it to do as a 120-pound adult. This includes jumping up on people, pushing through doorways and excessive barking. Bullmastiffs, as a breed, are fairly quiet, although a puppy reared with breeds that are generally noisy, such as Doberman Pinschers or Terriers, will bark more often than the Bullmastiff reared alone or with a quieter breed for a companion.

The Bullmastiff should have at the very least rudimentary obedience training as a puppy. This should include sit, down, stay, come and heel. This is true of any dog, but is especially important with a breed that regularly grows to 120 pounds.

Once a pup is housebroken and has learned the rudiments of good behavior, there are many more things to do with a Bullmastiff. Backpacking, camping, swimming, boating and carting are some informal pastimes that many fanciers enjoy with their dogs. Conformation showing, Obedience, performance events such as Tracking and Agility, and the Bullmastiff's work as a service dog will all be discussed in this book. If a Bullmastiff lacks for something to do, it is his owner's responsibility, not his own.

There's not much you can't do with a Bullmastiff.

A DEDICATED DOG

Bullmastiffs are strong, courageous, intelligent dogs, and have attracted admirers for more than a century. The dedication in Arthur Craven's 1932 book, *The Bull Mastiff As I Know It,* is quite touching and reflects upon the sterling character of the Bullmastiff. It reads:

This book is dedicated to Bell who was a Bull-Mastiff of the old type, a faithful animal and a wonderful mother. Bell's mistress had temporarily left her home to go on an errand, and a clothes-maiden, which was at

the front of the fire, presumably through vibration fell over and caused the house to be practically burnt down. Bell was in her kennel nursing puppies, but on seeing the flames she rushed forward, only to find the house closed. Hurtling herself at the door, she managed to break it open, and immediately rushed into the kitchen, where the owner's baby was lying in a pram; then, rearing herself up, she, with the gentleness of a mother, lifted the child out and carried it to safety, again returning to the house, this time presumably in search of her mistress. By her act of courage, through suffocation, Bell lost her life, but her faithful and courageous deed set for us an example of fidelity.

Bell was another of our canine heroines who answered the call of duty, faithful to the last. May her memory ever remain green!

Bullmastiffs are still sacrificing their lives for their family. I can relate an incident in the mountains of Kentucky in the spring of 1997. A mother allowed her two small children, ages three and four, to play outdoors while she and their father worked nearby. The family Bullmastiff, Cookie, watched over the children. A large rattlesnake was just out of hibernation, with its venom made even more deadly by constant distillation and concentration over the long winter. Cookie saw her duty and she did it, saving the children from harm. She killed the snake, but the venom took the brave dog's life. Cookie, like Bell, was a heroine. May their memory always remain green!

A PUPPY'S TALE

Since you bought this book, we'll assume you are among the breed's admirers. But before you go out and get a Bullmastiff, we'd like to tell you a story.

There was a sad young Bullmastiff in my backyard wondering where his family had gone. He was waiting for a new home because he simply was not the right dog for the family that purchased him when he was a small, cute puppy. From the start, he had a strong will and a dominant personality. His owners were quiet, unassertive and mild mannered. He was boisterous and wanted to run, play and chew.

His owners had a lovely home and many small, precious possessions that were very tempting to an energetic pup with new teeth erupting through his gums. He

Make sure you have the time and energy to cope with a big, boisterous dog.

wanted to play with the children but he didn't know how. He knocked the smaller ones down, and soon he wasn't allowed to play with them at all. He wanted to be petted and started jumping up on people to get the attention he craved. As a result, he was put out in the yard alone or was sent to his crate. One of his owners took him to obedience class, where he was a star pupil. Back at home he was still isolated from the rest of the family.

As he got bigger, he brought in more dirt on his feet, he got pimples on his face, he slobbered his water onto the floor around his bowl, and sometimes he drooled on people's clean clothes. He knocked the furniture over and was unruly in the house. He was even wilder outdoors, where he ate the shrubbery and destroyed the garden during his long hours alone.

The wife really never wanted a big dog at all, but she had agreed because her husband convinced her that he would take care of the dog and that it would be good for the children to have a pet. In the end, she was the one who put her foot down and said that the 120-pound, not-so-cute hulk had to leave. The people who sold them the puppy a year earlier were not interested in taking him back. He ultimately ended up in my backyard waiting for a new chance with a family willing to try to mold him into the pet he should have been all along.

THINGS TO CONSIDER

The very first questions a person should ask themself before committing to the purchase of a puppy of any breed are: Do I really have the time, patience, space and lifestyle to successfully raise a healthy, well-adjusted dog? Am I willing to take responsibility for a large dog for its entire life, which can be 10 years or more? Do I really want a strong-willed dog, and can I supply the balanced discipline and love to make him a good companion and not a plague on the neighborhood?

How long will the dog be expected to be alone each day? Is there someone at home during the day to take the puppy outdoors to relieve itself, or is there somebody who can keep it during

Perhaps a Bullmastiff is right for you. This is Tauralan Tequila Sunrise, NA, the first Bullmastiff to earn an Agility title. (Mona Lindau-Webb)

the day while I work? After a long day, do I have the energy and time to walk, train and play with a dog?

Do I have room for a pet that will weigh in excess of 100 pounds at maturity? Can I cope with drool, clean up accidents on the rug, go to training classes, and keep the dog clean and free of parasites? Can I afford a good-quality dog food, monthly heartworm preventive and other medications, and regular trips to the veterinarian for inoculations and checkups?

Are all the members of my household free of pet allergies? Is every member of the family agreeable to having a big dog in the house? On this last one, if the husband says yes and the wife says she'd really rather not, then don't get a Bullmastiff or any other breed until everyone in the family is fully committed to raising a dog and keeping it for life.

On the other hand, if you can answer yes to most of those questions, then perhaps a Bullmastiff is the dog for you.

Birthplace in Britain

B ritain, like other European countries, has hunting traditions that are very different from our customs in North America. There, wild game belonged to whoever owned the land. Hunting and fishing were not only sports for the squire, nobleman and king—their produce was a necessity for their tables.

THE GAMEKEEPER, THE POACHER AND THE NIGHT DOG

Poaching means illegally taking animals, wildfowl or fish on the property of another, and historically the punishment for poaching in Britain was severe. William the Conqueror (who died in 1087) decreed death for anyone caught poaching. Flogging and mutilation were not uncommon punishments in subsequent ages.

Transportation (a nice term for banishment) to Australia for seven years became the punishment for poaching in more enlightened times. The Game Laws, which began to be enforced with increasing violence after Napoleon's defeat at Waterloo in 1815, forbade anyone who was not a landowner with an annual worth of 100 pounds sterling, or a tenant for life with a rent of less than 150 pounds sterling, or the son or heir apparent of a squire or other person of higher rank, from taking game. Anyone else in possession of game was a poacher. It was not until the Human Rights and Social Justice Bill was passed in 1857 that the punishment for poaching was reduced to fines and imprisonment.

In this modern age we may wonder why the poacher risked such terrible retribution in order to take a rabbit or a pheasant. The answer is that life was always hard for the working man. The simple necessity of supplying his family with food forced some to take up poaching.

Still others poached for the money to be obtained from selling the game (as they still do). These poachers would arm themselves with a stout club and were often accompanied by a dog known as a Lurcher. Lurchers were obtained by breeding a Shepherd Dog to a Greyhound (it was done surreptitiously, as a Lurcher was definitely a poacher's dog). The Lurcher was an efficient helper. It was trained to slowly and quietly drive the quarry into a snare set on a game trail or into a long tangle-net stretched for several yards between bushes in a rabbit warren. A well-trained Lurcher and a long, silken tangle-net dyed to blend in with the surroundings could decimate a rabbit warren in one night. Lurchers were also trained to attack on command, if the poacher was accosted by a gamekeeper.

As humans have done through the ages, the gamekeeper turned to the dog for assistance. Various breeds of dogs were tried and found wanting. They were either too meek or too uncontrollable, too large and clumsy, or too small; or they

This child is well protected by two Bullmastiffs, not far removed from Night Dogs.

were not trainable for the task at hand. A cross between the English Mastiff and the old style English Bulldog was found to be the most suitable, yielding the Gamekeeper's Night Dog. The amount of each breed's blood in the Gamekeeper's Night Dog varied according to the preference of the particular keeper. Type—the physical characteristics that embody a breed standard—was of little concern to the gamekeeper, and size varied. However, the dogs rarely weighed much over 100 pounds.

We do not know the exact date when the Bullmastiff was created as a breed, since the gamekeepers kept no breeding records. Georges Louis Leclerc de Buffon, a French naturalist, wrote in his *Histoire Naturelle* in 1791, "The Bulldog produces with the Mastiff a dog which is called the Strong-Bulldog, and which is much larger than the real Bulldog, and approaching the Bulldog more than the Mastiff." Arthur Craven reproduced a newspaper advertisement in the second edition of his book *The Bull Mastiff as I Know It*, published in 1937. The advertisement, from the *Manchester*

Mercury, says, "Taken up on the road between Huddersfield and Marsden on Sunday 15 Nov. 1795 a large light coloured dog between the bull and mastiff kind." These are some of the earliest printed mentions of the Bullmastiff. One may be certain, however, that these were not the first or the only crossings of the Bulldog and Mastiff.

QUESTIONS OF TEMPERAMENT

Breed type was not important to the gamekeeper, who was interested only in performance. His Night Dog was created to fulfill his needs. It had to have a stable temperament, as it lived with his family. He certainly did not want his kin savaged or hurt.

The training of "demonstration" Night Dogs (dogs used in displays of tenacity and courage at exhibitions), such as the celebrated Thorneywood Terror, was not typical Night Dog training, although Terror's size at 90 pounds was considered ideal. Published reports of these exhibitions at the Crystal Palace in London describe the early equivalents of modern attack dogs—animals that were clearly unsuitable for use as a Gamekeeper's Night Dog. The Night Dog the keepers used had an altogether different training and was not a savage animal.

The true Night Dog had to have a quiet nature. This was required so as not to alert the poacher by growling or barking when the dog and the keeper were lying in wait. The dog had to be biddable (readily trained) so that it would attack on command. It had to be swift, agile and strong enough to overcome the Lurcher and still catch and pin the poacher. Finally, it had to be easily controlled so that it would release the poacher on command.

In addition, the innocent traveler had to be considered. The trespass laws in Britain are very different from those in the United States. There are public footpaths from one village to another, still in use today, that cross privately owned fields and woods. The gamekeeper could not have a dog that would attack these pedestrians. All this demands the utmost from a dog, and only the Bullmastiff was found to fit the bill.

It should be noted that the Bulldog was, by nature, a fierce dog. It was, by the 18th century, a breed that had survived the trials of bull, bear, lion-baiting and the dog pits. This was survival of the fittest in action. It was this fierceness and refusal to quit, when crossed with the Mastiff for size, that

A statue of an old-type Mastiff defending her litter. This monument graces the courtyard of Dorfold Hall, near Nantwich in England.

gave the gamekeeper an animal that met all his requirements.

The gamekeepers bred litters only when they needed them and culled ruthlessly, keeping only the best one or two puppies. This rigorous breeding program fixed those qualities that the gamekeeper required. We later-day fanciers may be thankful that the gamekeeper was so successful.

A RESPONSIBILITY PASSED ON

The Bullmastiff breed was developed by humans. The manufacture of this dog involved the deliberate selection of physical and mental characteristics that were deemed necessary to fulfill a particular need. These characteristics define the breed today and are to be cherished by modern fanciers.

Two British breeds, the hound-like English Mastiff and the old-style English Bulldog were used in this creation. These breeds, which many historians think are variants of an ancient common breed, had been interbred from time to time over the centuries, and their genetic pool was originally quite similar. The black chevron on the upper tail of a few Bullmastiffs is still regarded by some fanciers as indicative of genes inherited from ancestral Mastiff-Bulldog progenitors. However, today's Mastiff and Bulldog are quite unlike the Mastiff and Bulldog that were used to create the Bullmastiff. That means *if the Bullmastiff is allowed to be lost, it can never be re-created.*

THE PARENT BREEDS

The Mastiff and the Bulldog, at the time they were melded into the Bullmastiff, were themselves cursed with problems brought on by well-intentioned fanciers who had crossed in various foreign dogs. It seems to have been accepted practice among dog fanciers in the 19th century to experiment with trying to improve a breed by introducing a cross.

The Mastiff

The Mastiff had almost been lost in the 1700s, but survived when a few fanciers became alarmed and decided to resurrect the breed. The numbers at that time were so few that other breeds were used to increase the Mastiff population to a survivable level. It had just again reached the status of a definable breed in the early 1800s.

In his classic book *History of the Mastiff*, published in 1886, Reverend M. B. Wynn expressed his concern with the crossbreeding being used in this resurrection. Wynn and other early writers mentioned the use of many breeds that either no longer exist or are much changed today: the Alpine Mastiff, the Spanish Mastiff, the Bloodhound, the Newfoundland and the Bull & Mastiff. Their use in the Mastiff is still evidenced by faults, such as incorrect head and size, fluffy coat, gay tail (a tail carried above the horizontal), light eyes, liver mask and weak muzzle that plague the breed today. Because of these crosses, breeders came to regard any color other than fawn, apricot (red) or brindle as an indicator of impure blood.

The breed once again fell on hard times in the late 19th century when it became unfashionable to own a Mastiff. Numbers fell to the point where only 15 were registered in 1897, 24 in 1898 and 18 in 1899. An alarm was again raised, and a second attempt was made to save the breed. The early 1900s saw an enormous amount of cross-breeding with the Regency Bulldog to create the Bull Mastiff, and then breeding the Bull Mastiff back to a Mastiff. The Kennel Club opened its registry to the crossbred Bull Mastiff around 1900. This crossbreeding of the Mastiff quickly increased the numbers of dogs available as breeding stock, and by 1920 there were few Mastiffs that did not have a touch of the Bull.

The Mastiffs used to form the modern Bullmastiff usually weighed around 175 pounds. In a 1927 advertising pamphlet, Samuel E. Moseley, considered the father of the modern Bullmastiff, was careful to point out that the old-type English Mastiff he used in forming his Hamil and Farcroft dogs was more like a hound than the Mastiffs of the early 20th century. There was a much greater variance in type than we find in the breed today, as evidenced in the paintings of early Mastiffs.

As Moseley pointed out, the breed changed from a houndlike dog to the broader-skulled dog we see today. Regardless of how it was done, the Mastiff was saved and numbers were once again on the increase when the shadow of Hitler fell across Europe. The Mastiff population was swiftly decimated. After the war, the Mastiff population was so low that there was some crossbreeding to Bullmastiffs, and a red-brindle dog from the Harbex Kennel in Kent (a Bullmastiff kennel), found wandering after a blitz, was registered as a Mastiff and became an influential sire. The dog was registered as Templecombe Taurus, the name engraved on the collar he was wearing when he was found.

The old houndlike Mastiff of the type Moseley used in creating his Farcroft Bullmastiffs.

There has been quite a controversy surrounding this dog, with some adamant that he was a Mastiff and others just as adamant that he was a Bullmastiff. Elizabeth J. Baxter, writing in her book *The History and the Management of the Mastiff*, prints a letter written to her by Frances Warren of Harbex Bullmastiffs in which Warren states, "Harbex Tina had a litter in 1938 and a brindled bitch puppy (Lydia of Harbex) was sold to a Mrs. Button of Bexhill. Mrs. Button mated her to Ch. Springwell Major and Templecombe Taurus was the result." Hearing of the dog, Warren approached the secretary of the Old English Mastiff Club, told her of the dog's genealogy and left it up to her as to whether these facts should be divulged. The secretary, in what she saw as the best interests of the survival of the Mastiff breed, chose to continue to allow Taurus to be considered a Mastiff. Warren also says she later saw the dog being exhibited as a Mastiff and had a quiet chuckle to herself. It is somewhat gratifying to think that the Bullmastiff gave back to one of its parent breeds the ability to prosper.

Mastiff breeders are to be commended for the great advances made in the quality of their breed and for their perseverance in resurrecting the breed after World War II.

The Bulldog

The Bulldog, originally developed to bait bulls in a "sport" ring, also had its problems with purity. The Spanish Bulldog (a 100-pound dog) was interbred with the Bulldog, as were the Mastiff and various Terriers. The liver-colored pigmentation of the nose and lips that we call dudley, and that takes its name from the Bulldog Ch. Lord Dudley, whelped in 1877, no doubt came from the Spanish Bulldog.

The old-time bull baiters abhorred certain colors, such as black, black and tan, and blue. These colors were considered a sign of impure blood. The first Bulldog standard, known as the *Philo-Kuon Standard of 1865,* gave the allowed colors as "salmon, fallow, red, brindled, or white, with these colours variously

Ch. Springwell Major. This dog was of great influence not only in Bullmastiffs in Britain, the United States and Canada, but also in Mastiffs, where he helped rejuvenate the breed. He was later exported to the DeBeers Diamond Mining Company in South Africa.

pied. The salmon and fallow with black muzzles, called 'Smuts,' are choice colours. Some greatly admire the white, but a bright salmon with black muzzle would be the choicest of all colours."

Around the end of the 19th century, a craze for Toy Bulldogs swept England. Pugs had been brought to England by soldiers returning from the Siege of Peking in 1860, and they were crossed with the Bulldog to reduce its size. These Toy Bulldogs were eventually replaced by the French Bulldog.

There is still a problem in Bulldogs today with correct size, coming down from some of the early crosses. The original Bulldog standard of 1865 cautioned breeders that any Bulldog weighing more than 60 pounds "may be suspected of the Mastiff cross," and that "he ought not to be less than 20 lbs in weight, or he may be suspected of being crossed with the Terrier." These two crosses evidently were the main concern of Bulldog breeders in the 19th century.

Yet despite these warnings, in their zeal for the Bulldog the fanciers of the day evidently had no ethical problems with introducing crosses into other breeds. In fact, the same standard recommends the Bulldog to other canine fanciers "as very valuable to cross with Terriers, Pointers, Hounds, Greyhounds, etc., to give them courage and endurance."

The true Bulldog of the day was known as the Regency Bulldog, and it was this breed that was used to create the modern Bullmastiff. This Bulldog had only its great courage in common with the modern show ring breed. (It is a lasting shame that breeders in the 20th century have changed the Regency Bulldog into a caricature of the original.) It resembled, in body, the American Staffordshire Terrier and measured about 18 inches at the withers (the top of the shoulder), with the ideal weight for the bull-baiting dog listed as around 20 to 30 pounds.

There are considerable admonitions in early literature about not allowing the Bulldog to become too large. The portrait of Ball, owned by Mr. Lovell, is cited by the author of the *Philo-Kuon Standard* as showing ideal proportions. The painting reveals a dog much removed from the modern-day

Two Regency-type Bulldogs.

Bulldog. The head piece was a stronger-muzzled version of the modern Boxer head.

THE GAMEKEEPER'S NIGHT DOG

Writers on the Gamekeeper's Night Dog, the forerunner of the Bullmastiff, also decried undesirable crosses. In the case of the Night Dog, some of those crosses had been to the Great Dane, Bull Terrier and Bloodhound.

Modern Bullmastiff fanciers are sometimes defensive about the idea that other breeds, in addition to the pure Mastiff and the Bulldog, were used to create the Bullmastiff. However, many of these crosses were well documented. Moseley wrote in a February 11, 1927, *Dog World* article, "Still, we are not yet clear of either the Great Dane type or the crossbred." Douglas Oliff, in *The Mastiff and Bullmastiff Handbook,* has a very fine photograph of a Bullmastiff born before the breed was registered, Osmaston Turk, whose dam, Oliff states, was half Bloodhound and half Mastiff. The first standard for the breed cautions against Great Dane–type heads and Bull Terrier–type tails.

Moseley wrote in the early 1900s, "Type at present varies somewhat, and appears to follow a fashion in different districts. The mastiff has been used too much in the south to get size; in the north bull-dog blood predominates; while in the Nottingham and Derby districts, the great Dane has been extensively used, and many of the dogs from these districts show this most undesirable cross." Other writers, such as Arthur Craven, as well as newspaper advertisements of the era, bear witness to crosses with other breeds. We must remember that the gamekeeper was interested only in performance, not looks, and accept the fact that undesirable crosses were made.

Breeders, from the very start, worked and are still working to breed out the undesirable legacies of these crosses. Excessive wrinkle, apple skulls (domed topskull), loaded shoulders (excessive development of the muscles over the shoulder blades) with heavy fronts and light rears from the Bulldog, gay tails from the Bloodhound, and lack of substance and incorrect heads from the Great Dane may yet be encountered occasionally in the modern Bullmastiff.

Not all traces of these crosses are undesirable. It is quite possible that the celebrated oxblood-mahogany coat color of Doris Mullin's Mulorna line came from one of these early crosses. Modern breeders are now working hard to preserve this color.

A HISTORY RECORDED

There has been very little written about the formation of the Gamekeeper's Night Dog, and it must be remembered when searching old accounts of dog breeds that the authors of these accounts at times presented conjecture and theories as if they were facts. Therefore, care must be taken when forming opinions based on these old writings.

We owe a considerable debt to Eric Makins, the great historian of the breed. Makins, who became a fancier around the time the breed was recognized in Britain in 1924, collected stories from old gamekeepers. He wrote in *The American*

Bullmastiff Magazine in 1969, "Firstly I would say that . . . there were only few people who had the aptitude or opportunity to educate and breed dogs in this manner. Bullmastiffs were never as plentiful, as for example, any of the various breeds of terriers. The purposes for which they were used did not require that they should be bred in any great numbers, and moreover, the outlets were not numerous. This coupled with the fact that their training had to commence almost from the nest and to be on individual lines, meant that one man and one only was the teacher."

We find, by researching old tomes, that the first phase of training of the Night Dog was not unlike the training we do today with the pup we intend to keep as a house dog and companion. Each day, the puppy was taught to follow its master about for periods of longer and longer duration. It was encouraged to play with the keeper's other dogs, such as his terriers and retrievers, but it was not allowed to fraternize with strange dogs. The puppy was socialized with the ordinary animals around a farm, such as poultry, sheep and cattle.

Next, the puppy was taken into the woods and taught not to chase rabbits, pheasant and deer. Ignoring game was most essential, because the Night Dog's job was the single-minded apprehension of the poacher. A working Bullmastiff that was loosed and began chasing rabbits or fowl that had been disturbed by the poacher, instead of the poacher himself, was totally useless.

The puppy, from the start, was encouraged to cross any water he came across and to climb or jump any wall, fence or hedge. This is where the more cumbersome English Mastiff fell short.

A pair of Bullmastiffs from the late 1920s.

The next phase in the dog's training came at around six to nine months. This involved getting the dog used to wearing a muzzle. Makins writes that only the best and softest leather was used in these muzzles. Some muzzles were fitted with a leather throat guard for added protection during set-tos with the poacher's Lurcher.

Once the dog had become used to the muzzle, the "man-work" began. The gamekeeper and the dog would go for a walk in the woods. They would "surprise" a man waiting for them, who would immediately flee. The dog would be encouraged to chase the fleeing man. When the dog caught up to the man, the man would fall to the ground at the slightest touch from the animal. The keeper would be right there, urging the dog to "get him." This would continue until the dog chased the fugitive and knocked him down. It was

at this work that the keeper found the Bulldog lacking in essential substance and size.

At this point in training, the "fugitive" would start carrying a stick and would poke the dog as an irritant. The fun and games, as most Bullmastiffs previously regarded the chase, quickly changed and the dog would become keen and ferocious in his work. The sticks became larger and the blows harder, but by this time, through constant repetition, the dog had been taught that sticks or any similar weapons were not things to be feared, but obstacles to be disposed of as quickly as possible. (In the authors' experience training Bullmastiffs, the trick has not been in getting the dogs to turn on, but teaching them to turn off on command.)

The dog was also taught to ignore gunfire. The fleeing "fugitive" would stop and fire a small-caliber firearm into the air and then resume his flight. The dog would be encouraged to ignore the gunshot and to continue its pursuit. The caliber of the gun would be gradually increased, until the dog would ignore the loudest possible gunshot.

Flushing a hidden poacher was also taught. And in yet another facet of the training, the gamekeeper would take the dog into the woods at night and hide in a covert. A person posing as a poacher would then appear, and the dog would be trained to remain silent, making no sudden moves or vocal alarms until directed by the keeper.

The aim was to have a fully trained dog by the age of 18 months. Most important of all, however, the finished dog had to be controllable. Makins writes, "[A]lthough a dog was wanted that would attack at sight any man or object that approached out of the night, it always had to be under control.

Again, an animal that was so fierce that it would down even other keepers' dogs was not desired. The newcomer had to be trained to discriminate and it was therefore only when bidden that it moved and then continued with its work until called off, but the most important feature that had to be fostered was that once having been given the word 'go' that there was no turning back."

This temperament trait was a heritage from the Bulldog. Most Night Dogs would fight until death in defending their masters, and some certainly did. It was not unknown for a keeper to lose his life on some dark night out in the woods or on the moors. Makins also writes that bitches were often the choice of gamekeepers who worked alone, because a poacher would often secure a bitch in season and take it along on his errand in hopes of distracting the Night Dog. This ruse invariably failed when the Night Dog was a bitch.

The embodiment of all these qualities was Bess, a bitch whose exploits were described by Jack Barnard in an advertising booklet titled *A Gamekeeper Saved by his Night Dog*.

Bess, a Bull-Mastiff bitch belonging to Mr. W. Humphrey, Glack Park, Horsford, Norwich, tackled a dangerous poacher and in all probability saved her master's life. Bess . . . was a true type of Bull-Mastiff, a dark brindle in colour, of medium height and weighing eighty pounds. She downed the poacher no less than twenty times, it being impossible for him to get away from her.

In this particular instance the bitch Bess accompanied two keepers who were night watching, and, although the poachers could clearly be seen coming down the main ride in the moon light, and eventually

stopped within three yards of the keepers, who were concealed in a clump of trees, . . . the bitch did not move a limb or even whimper, although the poachers could be heard distinctly whispering. She steadily kept her place with the watchers and not until they emerged from their hiding place, when the poachers were about to shoot a pheasant and were challenged by the head-keeper, did the bitch give the slightest sign.

Instantly the men bolted and the bitch in pursuit. She downed the man who had the gun and kept him there until the keeper arrived on the spot. The other man got away during the struggle, but the bitch went after him and overtook him and was worrying him when the keeper arrived on the spot. The poacher begged for the bitch to be called off, which the keeper did. When the man regained his feet he flew at the keeper, both going to the ground, the poacher on top. However, the bitch pinned the poacher through the arm, and the keeper then dealt with him. The work done by Bess in this very bad case was wonderful.

It should be noted that these Night Dogs rarely weighed more than 110 pounds. The over-boned, clumsy and heavy specimens that weigh upwards of 140 pounds seen in the show ring today would have been rejected by the gamekeeper as totally unsuitable for the work.

THE BULLMASTIFF BECOMES A PUREBRED

The sport of dog showing is responsible for most breeds remaining pure and for the Bullmastiff reaching the status of a purebred. The need to keep correct records of the dogs exhibited at shows is the reason organizations that register dogs and promulgate dog show rules were established.

For many of the working breeds, the first dog shows were agricultural fairs, where dogs were exhibited like other valuable livestock. Some dog fanciers have suggested that the first dog shows were the blood sports, such as bull and bear baiting and the fighting pit, or perhaps the rat-killing contests of the terriers.

The first dog shows that in any way resemble the dog shows we know today took place in the early 1850s. These shows were generally held in pubs. The Kennel Club in Britain makes the claim that the 1855 painting by R. Marshall titled *A dog show, lead, or match at Jemmy Shaw's public house* depicts the first dog show. Lyn Pratt, in her 1996 book *Bullmastiffs Today*, cites even earlier ones.

What were these early shows like? An interesting article by J.E., writing in *The Illustrated Kennel Club News*, October 29, 1911, describes "the first organized dog show which ever took place," held at the Town Hall in Newcastle-on-Tyne on June 28 and 29, 1859. "Competition was confined to Pointers and Setters, and there were sixty entries, with three judges to each breed. This show was the precursor of others in various parts of the kingdom, but they were not numerous, as we understand shows now, and were run on very easygoing lines under their own rules, which were often very lax. There was no registration in those days, and a dog could be entered at different shows under various names, and one dog substituted for another, and various other evils obtained."

The Bullmastiff, still being considered cross-bred in those days, was not offered a class at these early shows. Eventually the gamekeepers organized their own shows, the first of which was held at the Aquarium on August 1, 1900.

The shows continued off and on in the early 1900s, and included exhibitions of the Bullmastiff's prowess in downing and keeping down a strong man while securely muzzled. The dogs were working Night Dogs, and size and type varied greatly. For the most part, the dogs were smaller and lighter than today's Bullmastiffs, standing 22 to 26 inches and weighing 70 to 100 pounds, with little or no fat.

Ch. Bartonville Red Sultan, one of Tom Pennington's dogs from the 1920s.

Thorneywood Terror, the most celebrated of the Bullmastiffs used in these man-versus-dog exhibitions, weighed 90 pounds. It is claimed that no man ever escaped him. Terror was owned and trained by William Burton of Thorneywood Kennels, Nottinghamshire. The influence of this man and his dogs on the breed was tremendous. The first prizewinners at the Gamekeepers Annual Dog Shows from 1901 to 1906 were all either Thorneywood bred or were sired by a Thorney-wood dog. Terror was also an influence in the Mastiff breed; several Mastiffs registered during this time listed him as the sire. Burton, in common with many early Bullmastiff breeders, also bred Mastiffs, and it was not unusual to find Mastiffs with a Bullmastiff ancestor and vice-versa in Kennel Club registrations.

J. D. Biggs of Osmaston Hall in Derbyshire was another early and influential breeder of both Bullmastiffs and Mastiffs, under the Osmaston banner. Derbyshire evidently was plagued with poach-ers, because Biggs bragged that two of his Night Dogs had taken more poachers between them than had been taken in all the rest of England.

Jack Barnard told a story about Biggs: "Some years ago Mr. Biggs was set upon by poachers one night and desperately attacked. It was a melee, and a struggle for life on the ground. His Bull-Mastiff bitch, Osmanton Daisy, though terribly knocked about, outed the three poachers in the end, and, during the whole of the struggle, she stepped over and about her master's body like a lamb."

Samuel E. Moseley of Farcroft Kennels in Stoke-on-Trent arrived on the Bullmastiff scene sometime around 1910 and immediately started working toward full recognition by the Kennel Club. (Moseley also sometimes used the kennel name Hamil.) He also bred Mastiffs, and it should be remembered that while some of the Mastiffs of this period already carried considerable Bulldog blood, Moseley claimed to have used the old houndlike Mastiff. This is probably true, as the Mastiff Ch. Crown Prince had been used heavily by this time to broaden skulls and shorten muzzles in the show ring Mastiff of Moseley's day. Unfortunately, Crown Prince also brought the structural faults and clumsiness that are still seen today.

Farcroft heads and structure certainly reflected the use of the older hound type of Mastiff. An article by Will Hally in the December 1924 issue of *Our Dogs* described Moseley's dogs: "The Bull-mastiffs at Farcroft, are 60 per cent Mastiff and 40 per cent Bull. They are 27 to 28 inches at the shoulder and weigh 90 to 110 pounds. There is no Boarhound or Great Dane blood in them, and nothing of the first cross Mastiff and Bull, nor are they weedy mastiffs. They have wonderful noses and will track down and hold a man on command, but are neither ferocious or quarrelsome and are not aggressive."

The 60-40 ratio of Mastiff to Bulldog was highly publicized by Moseley as his "formula," and it is often widely but unwisely quoted by novices in the breed today. Moseley supplied Bullmastiffs to John Cross, who wrote the first American standard in 1935. Cross included Moseley's ratio, and it was picked up by the Canadians when they adopted their first standard.

Moseley understood the benefits of advertising and was not shy about trumpeting the wins and virtues of his dogs. He also was successful in recruiting writers to publish favorable reviews in the dog press.

Despite the publicity, Moseley and the other pioneers were not to have success with their

One of the few surviving photographs of Moseley, accompanied by an early Bullmastiff. This photo was taken in 1924.

campaign for breed recognition until the end of 1924. The Kennel Club published the good news in the *K. C. Gazette* on December 24, 1924. Bullmastiffs were to be judged in the "Any Other Variety" section, but were eligible for a place in the Register of Breeds. It set out the prerequisites, "It is, of course, most important to observe the distinction between a Bull-Mastiff (pure bred) and a Bull-Mastiff (cross bred), the former being a dog with both parents and the preceding three generations all Bull-Mastiffs with out the introduction of a Mastiff or Bulldog. The term Bull-Mastiff (cross bred) implies the existence of a definite cross which has not yet been bred out. . . ." It took just under three years for the requirements to be met. Full registration was granted in October 1927, and the breed was allotted four sets of Challenge Certificates for 1928.

The growth and development of the breed in Britain were rapid after admission to the ranks of the purebred in 1924. The number of registrations began quickly increasing from a start of 63 in 1925 to 584 registered in 1935, just 10 years later. The long climb toward consistency in breed type had begun.

The Bullmastiff's history in the dog show ring properly began August 6, 1925, when one class was scheduled for the breed at the Bagnall Open Show in Staffordshire. This must have been an interesting show for R. T. Baines to judge, as there was no standard in existence to guide him at the time. Moseley's fawn dog, Farcroft Fidelity, was awarded the win. Farcroft Fidelity's measurements are given by Moseley as 28 inches and 116 pounds.

(G. Slater)

CHAPTER 3

The Breed Standard and What It Means

The modern Bullmastiff developed in Britain from the early Gamekeeper's Night Dogs. The dogs that served as the foundation of the breed were those that possessed the necessary behavior and temperament, coupled with the stature and strength to perform as essential working partners with the gamekeepers. Dogs were often selected for behavioral traits that made them an asset to the gamekeeper: great courage, dedication to their master, the ability to detect danger or threat, trainability, the sense to refrain from unnecessarily vicious behavior or mauling, reliability and a dependable temperament. These men were more interested in dogs that could and would protect them in their sometimes dangerous occupation, and less interested in general appearance.

As the Gamekeeper's Night Dogs became known for their outstanding working abilities, fanciers and keepers alike began to recognize that certain physical characteristics were present in the finest of the working stock and that those traits contributed to the function and performance of the dog. Eventually those attributes were written down, and the first standard was conceived in 1925. From that point onward, the Bullmastiff began its journey toward standardization in appearance, as well as performance and temperament.

21

The written standard of the breed sets down in words a picture of what constitutes an ideal Bullmastiff: structure, size, head, body, coat, color, gait and temperament. There are three similar but separate major standards for the Bullmastiff: the one approved by the American Kennel Club most recently in 1992, the standard from the Canadian Kennel Club, and the British standard approved by the Kennel Club in 1994. Since the British standard is from the country where the breed originated, it is the one most widely accepted by other countries and by the Fédération Cynologique Internationale, the governing body for most international dog shows.

EARLY STANDARDS

When Bullmastiffs were first recognized in Britain, they were, at best, a very mixed lot, and disagreements abounded among the first breed clubs concerning just what should be included in the standard for the breed.

A very early dog show, with Bullmastiffs of various types and sizes. (Phyllis Robson)

The Midland Bullmastiff Club was the first association of fanciers, and at their general meeting at Derby on September 4, 1925, they adopted the first breed standard. It said:

HEAD: To be square and compact; on no account to be long or of the Great Dane type. Muzzle to be square. Head and fairly short neck to be set on fairly well set up shoulders. Ears on no account to be large and drooping, but rather to be of a size between the Bulldog and the Mastiff, showing an alert expression when dog excited or aroused. Eye to be preferably dark, although a hazel eye must not be considered a bar provided the dog confirms to type. Slight haw not altogether detrimental. An undershot mouth not to be a bar in view of the fact of the dog's breeding. Wrinkle on skull desirable, but not essential.

BODY: Chest to be muscular and broad. To be well-ribbed-up and not too long. Even proportions to be aimed at. Dog must not be too leggy. Legs must be straight. Tendency towards cow hocks or bowed front to be avoided. Tail must be thick at the top, gradually tapering, but not too fine as in the case of the Bull Terrier. Gay tail carriage a decided drawback. A cranked tail is not to be a bar, although the eventual type might be improved by having a straight tail. The Bulldog type of cranked tail is bound to appear from time to time. Coat must be hard and short, similar in texture to the Mastiff or Bulldog. A shaggy coat is a decided disqualification.

COLOUR: To be fawn or brindle: any shade of fawn or brindle permissible. Black masks preferable. Slight white marking on chest or toes not to be a detriment, but patches of white on body to be avoided. Breeders to remember that a dog with a poor body and a good head is quite as bad as one with a poor head and a good body.

GENERAL FEATURES: To be aimed at in the make-up of a Bull Mastiff should be courage, activity, and strength. The dog's disposition should be cheerful, and shyness the very first thing to be avoided. Intelligence must always be kept in view. The type of dog is naturally intelligent and by careful breeding and training such intelligence can be developed very strongly.

SIZE OF DOG: Bitches, 75 to 90 lb. weight, height at shoulder 23/25 in. Dogs, 90 to 110 lb. weight, height at shoulder 24/26 in. The big outstanding type of dog is to be avoided. Breeders to remember that they are not to aim at producing a dog as big as the Mastiff.

Prizdor King, a Bullmastiff of this early British type.

Soon after that standard was written, the National Bull-mastiff Police-Dog Club was formed. Samuel Moseley was the driving force behind this club, which promptly adopted its own standard.

In general appearance the Bull-mastiff is a noble symmetrical animal with well-knit frame, powerful and active, courageous but docile.

Dogs should be 25 to 27 inches at shoulder and 90 to 110 lbs. in weight. Bitches 80 to 90 lbs. and 24 to 26 inches.

The head should be large and square with fair wrinkle. Muzzle not more than 3½ inches long, deep and broad. Flews not too pendulous, stop moderate, mouth level, favour projection of the lower rather than the upper incisors. Canine teeth large and set wide. Eyes dark and of medium size set apart the width of muzzle with furrow between. Dark mask preferable. Skull large and may measure almost equal the height of the dog; it should be broad with cheeks well developed. Forehead flat, ears V or folded back, set on wide and high, level with occiput and cheek, giving a square appearance to the skull.

Chest wide and deep, well set down between forelegs. Girth may be up to a third more than the dog's height. Ribs arched, deep and well set back to hips.

Back short, giving a compact carriage. Shoulders muscular and slightly sloping. Arms powerful, elbows square, forelegs straight, feet large with round toes well arched. Loins wide and muscular, slightly arched with fair depth of flank. Hind legs broad and muscular with well developed second thigh denoting power but not cumbersome. Hocks, bent "cow hocks" or splay feet are most undesirable. Tail set high up, strong at root and tapering, reaching to or just below the hocks—straight or curved but never carried gay or hound fashion.

Coat short and dense, giving good weather protection. Colour, any shade fawn or brindle.

These two standards were in effect at the same time, and we can pity the poor exhibitors who entered a show not knowing by which standard their dogs would be judged!

Although they could boast of having put on the first show exclusively for the breed, the Midlands Club ceased to exist after only two years. The British Bullmastiff League was organized with some of the members from the former Midlands Club in 1931, but eventually Moseley and the National's standard won out, and for awhile that club reigned supreme. The National Police Dog Club sponsored the first Bullmastiff classes at Crufts.

Subsequently, the tables were turned. The British Bullmastiff League adopted a standard that soon superseded that of the National. The League standard called for dogs to be 25 to 27 inches and 90 to 110 pounds, with bitches to be 24 to 26 inches and 80 to 90 pounds. These weights were changed, not without controversy, in 1937 to 100 to 125 pounds for dogs 90 to 110 pounds for bitches.

The Southern Bullmastiff Society, formed in 1935, kept the heavier weights in their standard, written in 1943. The British Bullmastiff League increased the dog weight, in 1956, to the 130 pounds we have today.

Many of the pioneering breeders were unhappy with these increases in allowable weight.

Eric Makins, who wrote the second book ever written on the breed, *The Bullmastiff*, also wrote in *Our Dogs* magazine in December 1949,

I have been extremely interested in the opinions of correspondents concerning the alterations in the breed standard, which have been agreed upon by the various clubs, and on the views of some of them about the dogs of the pre-recognition era. Several of the older breeders, including Mrs. Mullin and Mr. Jack Barnard, have pointed out the danger of oversize both as regards bulk and height. When framing a standard for a large breed, you have obviously got to be elastic and allow a maximum and a minimum for height and weight. It would seem, however, that the weight allowance of 130 pounds opens the door to the oversize dog. . . . As Mr. Barnard rightly points out, if you allow 130 pounds, then you are going to get 140 pounds and 150 pounds and then you are right among the Mastiffs. I don't think that either Mrs. Mullin or Mr. Barnard or anyone else for that matter, suggested that dogs of Mastiff type were winning today, although I think that there are some who are very near it, but what they wished to stress was the fact that if the 130 pound limit is persisted in, then the way is open for the Mastiff type.

If he were still alive today, Makins would be pleased to find that the modern British breeders have exercised caution, and that there are very few Bullmastiffs in Britain that approach the Mastiff in type or stature.

Unfortunately, his prophecy, at least in regard to size, has been fulfilled in the United States. It is not unusual to see several of the mature dogs in the show ring exceeding one or the other of the standard's limit of 27 inches and 130 pounds. However most of these dogs, some of which may reach 28 inches and/or 150 pounds, do not appear to resemble the Mastiff in type. Rather they look like giant, over-boned Bullmastiffs.

With so many over-sized dogs, it is surprising to find that the bitches are at the lower end or below the limits of the standard. I attribute this problem to the fact that we have only a small number of breeder-judges in the United States. Most often the breed is adjudicated by non-breeder judges, who seem only to remember part of the line in the American standard that reads, "Other things being equal, the more sub-stantial dog within these limits is favored." They ignore or forget the words "within these limits," which means within the limits of the standard: 25 to 27 inches, 110 to 130 pounds for dogs and 24 to 26 inches, 100 to 120 pounds for bitches.

American breeders would do well to forget the decisions of these modern all-rounders and take to heart the last, cautionary line of the first standard for the breed: "Breeders to remember that they are not to aim at producing a dog as big as the Mastiff."

A modern British champion, Honeybee of Olwell—feminine yet powerful.

THE FIRST AMERICAN STANDARD

The Bull-Mastiff Club of America was formed in 1935. There is no record of this club doing anything other than drafting a new standard. We could find no record of who founded the club, but it is more than probable that John Cross wrote the new standard. Samuel Moseley's influence on Cross may be seen by those familiar with Moseley's National Police Dog Club standard.

The newly drafted standard was approved by the American Kennel Club in 1935, replacing the ini-tial British Bullmastiff League Standard.

GENERAL APPEARANCE: The Bull-Mastiff is a sym-metrical animal, showing great strength, powerfully built but active. He is fearless yet docile, and has endurance and alertness. He is 60 percent Mastiff and 40 percent Bulldog.

SIZE: Dogs should be 25 to 27 inches at shoulder, and about 115 pounds in weight; bitches, 24 to 26 inches at shoulder, and about 100 pounds in weight.

HEAD: Skull—Large and square with fair wrinkle, and in circumference may measure almost the height of the dog; it should be broad with cheeks well developed. Forehead flat.

Muzzle—Should not be more than 3½ inches long, deep and broad. Nose, black, with nostrils large and broad. Flews not too pendulous, stop moderate, mouth preferably level, or may be slightly undershot. Canine teeth large and set wide. A dark mask is preferable.

Eyes—Dark and medium size, set apart, the width of the muzzle with furrow between.

Ears—Should be V-shaped and carried close to cheek or folded back, set on wide and high, level with occiput and cheek, giving a square appearance to the skull. They should be denser in color than the body, and of medium size.

BODY: Neck—Should be slightly arched, of moderate length, very muscular, and almost equal in circumference to skull.

Chest—Wide and deep, with ribs well sprung, well set down between fore legs. Girth may be up to a third more than dog's height.

Fore Quarters—Shoulders should be muscular and slightly sloping. Forelegs straight, well boned and set wide apart, elbows square.

Pasterns straight, feet medium, with round toes well arched, pads hard.

Back—Short, giving compact carriage.

COAT: Short and dense, giving good weather protection.

COLOR: Any shade of fawn or brindle.

A scale of points is not given, for in the last analysis, a dog is judged on his breed characteristics, and his soundness which is so essential in working breeds. Great harm can be done by breeding for certain characteristics, because of heavy point score, to the detriment of soundness. This, we wish to avoid.

Due to the relatively recent origin of this breed as a pure-bred type, it was thought well to explain in detail certain aims of the breeders of Bull-Mastiffs with which the standard should not be burdened.

Relative to the mouth, it is unreasonable to expect nothing but level mouths in a breed whose blood is made up of Bulldogs and Mastiffs. It is the desire of Bull-Mastiff breeders to produce, in time and by selective breeding, dogs with level mouths. This however, must be considered as secondary in importance to the production of sound dogs. The same is true of the dark mask and density of color of ear. As to the size, there are dogs with ears which are "sloppy," and there are those who show too much of the Bulldog ear. Here we want the happy medium and here, again, it is a refinement which must come after soundness and general type conformation. There is also the question of white tips, which has been debated at some length in the English canine press. It is maintained by some that this is from the Bulldog, and by others that it is Bullterrier blood, which certain unscrupulous breeders have used. Whatever it comes from, it should be eliminated as it has no part in the color scheme of our breed. White on the head or body is not tolerated.

As to the size of the breed, the reason for the creation of the Bull-Mastiff was the desire for a dog smaller than the old English Mastiff and more active, but one still big enough to throw and hold a man. Therefore a dog of 100 pounds who is sound and

"Sound, active dogs, capable of protecting life and property." This is Ch. Coomblome River Work.

active is greatly to be preferred to a dog of 125 pounds who looks like a weedy Mastiff. It is only in the case that these two animals are equal in all other respects, that the larger may be preferred. Again, if we see a dog weighing 140 or 150 pounds, even though sound and active, we then approach too much the Mastiff and the breed is losing identity.

To sum up, let us say that we want sound, active dogs, capable of protecting life and property, of throwing and holding a man. We want dogs conforming to breed-type and refinements will increase in importance in direct proportion to the attainment of the primary ideals.

This standard remained in effect until 1960, when the American Bullmastiff Association, the successor to the Bull-Mastiff Club of America, promulgated a new one. This was three years after the ABA was recognized by the American Kennel Club as the parent club of the breed.

It is the authors' opinion that little was gained in the new standard, other than size adjustments, and much guidance that was extremely valuable, both to breeders and judges, was lost.

COMPARING THE STANDARDS TODAY

Since every standard is really a description of an image, much can be learned from reading different standards and comparing how they have described what is, essentially, the same image—that of an ideal Bullmastiff.

THE AKC STANDARD

The American Kennel Club approved changes to the standard submitted by the American Bullmastiff Association, the parent club for the breed, on February 8, 1992. The amended standard went into effect March 31, 1992.

Geraldine M. Roach, a noted Bullmastiff judge, explains and expands on the points made in the standard. Her comments are in italics in between the pertinent sections of the standard. (The drawings in this section are all by Maren Phillips.)

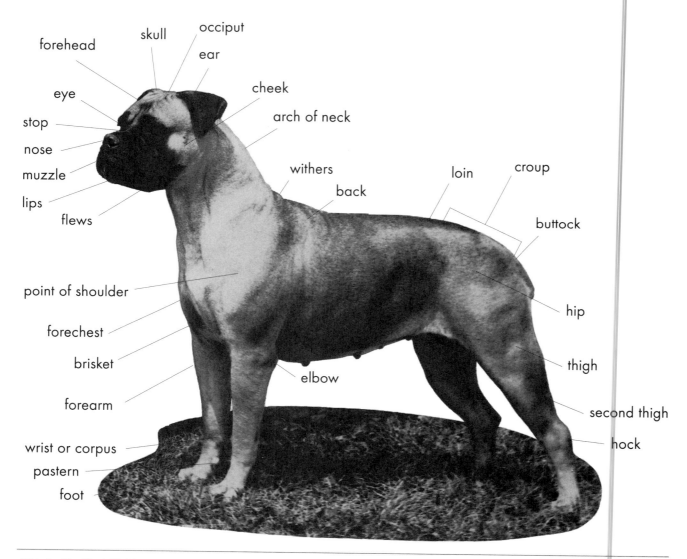

forehead
skull
occiput
ear
cheek
eye
stop
nose
muzzle
lips
flews
arch of neck
withers
back
loin
croup
buttock
point of shoulder
forechest
brisket
elbow
hip
thigh
forearm
second thigh
wrist or corpus
hock
pastern
foot

This is Ch. Myrick's Tomarrow (Black Knight's Caesar out of Scyldocga Queen Phillippa), an outstanding bitch of the 1960s. (E. H. Frank)

Official Standard for the Bullmastiff

GENERAL APPEARANCE—That of a symmetrical animal, showing great strength, endurance, and alertness; powerfully built but active. The foundation breeding was 60 percent Mastiff and 40 percent Bulldog. The breed was developed in England by gamekeepers for protection against poachers.

This introductory paragraph describes the overall physical impression of the Bullmastiff, the antecedents that gave it a unique type, and the purpose for which the breed was intended. In other words, it outlines a strong working dog and emphasizes structure, type and function. All three of these elements were present in the early Bullmastiff, as they are in Bullmastiffs today.

SIZE, PROPORTION, SUBSTANCE—*Size*—Dogs, 25 to 27 inches at the withers, and 110 to 130 pounds weight. Bitches, 24 to 26 inches at the withers, and 100 to 120 pounds weight. Other things being equal, the more substantial dog within these limits is favored. *Proportion*—The length from tip of breastbone to rear of thigh exceeds the height from withers to ground only slightly, resulting in a nearly square appearance.

Not a giant dog; the ideal height of the Bullmastiff has remained generally the same over the years in most written standards. The weight, however, has been increased since the first Bullmastiffs were registered, and is now also slightly greater for bitches than the current British standard permits. A premium is put on substance, within the limits of the standard, meaning muscle and bone rather than bulk and fat. This substance should never be at the expense of the required elements of power, endurance, agility and activity mentioned under General Appearance.

Although not actually one of the square breeds, the ideal Bullmastiff should always have a square appearance.

The closer a dog approaches a noticeably rectangular silhouette, the less correct it is on this point—an element that helps differentiate the breed from the Mastiff. A balanced Bullmastiff should have a deep body that is approximately one half of its total height at the withers (top of the shoulder). One should also remember that although width is not mentioned in this part of the standard, to be a "symmetrical" and "powerfully built" Bullmastiff, a dog should possess sufficient width to balance its height and length when viewed from any angle. When viewed from above, the width of the front, the ribs and the rear should be equal.

HEAD—*Expression*—Keen, alert, and intelligent. *Eyes*—Dark and of medium size. *Ears*—V-shaped and carried close to the cheeks, set on wide and high, level with occiput and cheeks, giving a square appearance to the skull; darker in color than the body and medium in size. *Skull*—Large, with a fair amount of wrinkle when alert; broad, with cheeks well developed. Forehead flat. *Stop*—Moderate.

A well-proportioned bitch. (American Kennel Club)

Muzzle—Broad and deep; its length, in comparison with that of the entire head, approximately as 1 is to 3. Lack of foreface with nostrils set on top of muzzle is a reversion to the Bulldog and is very undesirable. A dark muzzle is preferable. *Nose*—Black, with nostrils large and broad. *Flews*—Not too pendulous. *Bite*—Preferably level or slightly undershot. Canine teeth large and set wide apart.

The standard gives its greatest emphasis to the section on the head, for two reasons: because the head is composed of so many individual parts, and because a good head

identifies the dog as a Bullmastiff rather than a Bulldog, a Boxer or a small Mastiff.

Taken as a whole, the head should have a square appearance, just as should the overall body structure.

One of the characteristics the breed legitimately inherited from its Bulldog ancestors is a broad, shortened skull. The Bullmastiff lacks what is known in other breeds as backskull. This means that the occipital bone on a Bullmastiff is set between the ears, rather than extending to some point behind them, as in the Mastiff. Viewed from the top, the portion of the head from the stop (the step up from the muzzle to the point between the eyes) to the occiput (the highest and rearmost part of the skull) should roughly equal the width of the head from cheekbone to cheekbone, but not including the cheek muscles, which should also be clearly present on a good representative Bullmastiff head.

For symmetry, the head should be approximately as deep as it is wide, thus forming a padded cube. An old rule of thumb was that the circumference of the head, measured from a point in front of the ears, should be equal to or slightly greater than the height of the dog from ground to withers.

Ideally, the muzzle is to be broad and deep with a length in profile that is one third of the entire head from tip of the nose to the occiput—in other words, one-third muzzle, two-thirds head (skull length). The width of the muzzle should be approximately the same as the length and the depth, forming a padded block that is securely attached to the square head.

Some slight wrinkling across the muzzle may be permitted, but a Bullmastiff should never have so much nor so little wrinkle on the forehead that the expression and wrinkle pattern on the head does not change when the dog is alert and comes to full attention. This point is functional as well as aesthetic, because it serves as a form of communication between dog and owner, and has been prized since early gamekeepers' days.

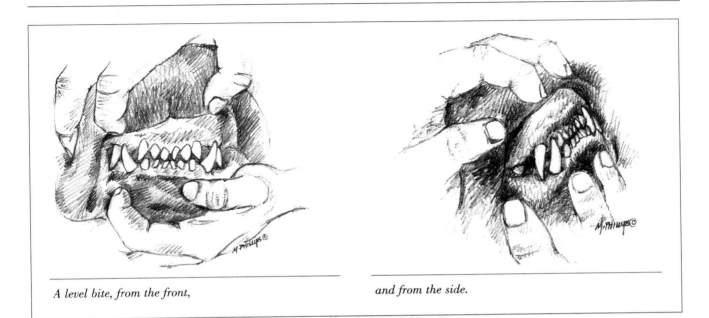

A level bite, from the front,

and from the side.

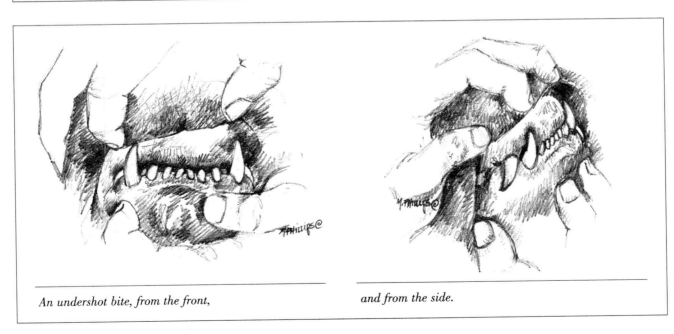

An undershot bite, from the front,

and from the side.

The dark, medium size eyes are set wide apart, to allow a full range of vision and to avoid injury to both at one time in a skirmish with man or beast. Cosmetically, they square off the center area of the face and contribute immensely to the keen, alert, intelligent expression.

Few faults are mentioned in the AKC standard, so when a particular characteristic is pointed out, it should be carefully noted: "Lack of foreface with nostrils set on top of muzzle is a reversion to the Bulldog and is very undesirable." This is not to be confused with a pugnacious chin resulting from an undershot jaw (where the front teeth of the lower jaw overlap or project beyond the front teeth of the upper jaw when the mouth is closed). To differentiate between the two, look at the angle of the nose as it departs from the bridge of the muzzle. In profile, if the front of the nose forms a 45-degree angle with the top line of the nose, it should not generally be considered a reversion to the Bulldog. A far more common nose fault in Bullmastiffs is small or pinched nostrils.

The mouth is broad and the canine teeth set wide to square off the jaw. It has been argued that the level bite (where the front teeth of the upper and lower jaws meet edge to edge) is not normally considered functional. In the case of the Bullmastiff, which was developed to knock down and hold a man without mauling or inflicting unnecessary injuries, this type of bite is indeed suited to the purpose. The very "inefficiency" of the level or slightly undershot bite allows a person to be held without much of the ripping or slashing often encountered with the scissors or pincer bite found in many of the herding or guarding breeds.

Excessive flews (the fleshy upper lips) would be a hindrance to a dog attempting to securely hold a struggling felon. Aesthetically, the deep, square lower muzzle should come from strength and depth of underjaw and not from an illusion created by floppy flews.

Ears are V-shaped and darker in color than the body. Although a dog may be forgiven for not possessing black

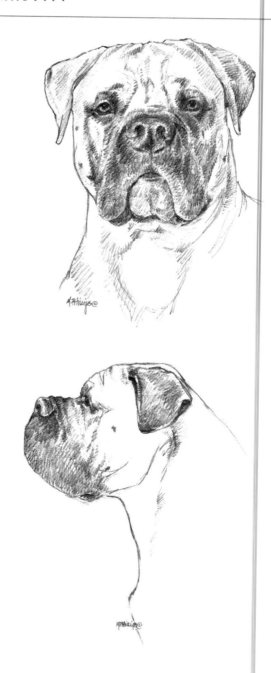

ears, the darker coloring should be preferred by breeders to
prevent loss of pigmentation on this point. When alert, the ears come forward slightly and frame the top half of the face. The ears should not be large, but rather in proportion to the head. Well set ears of correct size and shape greatly enhance the expression and contribute to the overall square look.

Although the AKC standard only remarks that the dark muzzle is preferred, it is probably best for breeders to strive for the black muzzle and masking considered essential by the British and Canadian standards. A Bullmastiff with a faded or absent mask departs from accepted breed type for showing or breeding, and ranges uncomfortably close to the coloration of the Dogue De Bordeau.

The head is therefore one of the signature characteristics of type in the Bullmastiff, and should never be such that there could be the slightest confusion with the Mastiff, Bulldog, Rhodesian Ridgeback, Dogue De Bordeau or any other breed.

The ears of an alert dog should frame the top half of the face, as they do on Aust. Ch. Nightwatch Lady Nikita. (Animal Pics)

NECK, TOPLINE, BODY—*Neck*—Slightly arched, of moderate length, very muscular, and almost equal in circumference to the skull. *Topline*—Straight and level between withers and loin. *Body*—Compact. Chest wide and deep, with ribs well sprung and well set down between the forelegs. *Back*—Short, giving the impression of a well balanced dog. *Loin*—Wide, muscular, and slightly arched, with fair depth of flank. *Tail*—Set on high, strong at the root, and tapering to the hocks. It may be straight or curved, but never carried hound fashion.

This section of the standard describes a thick, powerful, compact dog that is capable of working. Compactness and a short, level back are the keys to the ideal, well-balanced

Bullmastiff body. The tail is set on high, and should be an extension of the topline. Low-set tails have become commonplace, as well as equally incorrect rounded croups (the muscular area just above and around the set-on of the tail) more appropriate to coursing dogs. A sudden drop in the croup ruins the square outline and weakens the stability needed for the dog to keep its balance when subduing an intruder.

FOREQUARTERS—*Shoulders*—Muscular but not loaded, and slightly sloping. *Forelegs*—Straight, well boned, and set well apart; elbows turned neither in nor out. *Pasterns* straight, feet of medium size, with round toes well arched. *Pads* thick and tough, nails black.

HINDQUARTERS—Broad and muscular, with well developed second thigh denoting power, but not cumbersome. Moderate angulation at hocks. Cowhocks and splay feet are *serious faults.*

Although these opposite ends of the dog are treated separately in the standard, they must be considered together to achieve the proper balance and symmetry. Shoulders are slightly sloping to go with the strong, straight pasterns (wrist), and the moderate angulation at the hock (the rear joint between the ankle and the lower thigh). It is reasonable to assume that if the hocks are moderately bent, the stifles (knee joints) will be moderately angulated as well. Cowhocks (where the hocks turn in and the back feet toe out) and splay feet (flat feet with spreading toes) are designated as serious faults, and should not be tolerated. Although splay feet are mentioned under the heading of Hindquarters, they are an equally serious fault on the front feet. Similarly, thick, tough pads and black nails are not just requirements on the front feet. The dog is the sum of its parts and the way they fit together.

COAT—Short and dense, giving good weather protection.

A short, dense coat is less likely to collect mud and debris, and is less exposed to the elements than a longer, slightly open one. The British penalize long, silky and woolly coats in their standard and require the haircoat to lie flat against the body. The AKC standard simply states what is acceptable, and expects common sense to exclude the occasional longhaired Bullmastiff from the show ring and the breeding program.

COLOR—Red, fawn, or brindle. Except for a very small white spot on the chest, white marking is considered a fault.

Although brindle (a pattern in which black is striped and layered with a lighter color) was the color preferred by early gamekeepers, for many years brindle dogs were at a disadvantage in the show ring. But in the past decade many serious breeders have made concentrated efforts to produce outstanding brindle Bullmastiffs. As a result, they are seen in increasing numbers every year.

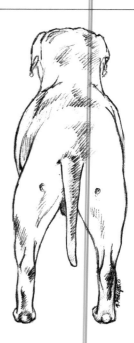

Solid fawns and reds should ideally have clear, even colored coats.

White markings are a fault in all Bullmastiff standards, and should be penalized to the extent of the marking. A large amount of white is a larger fault, but unless extensive, it should never be considered with the same severity as splayed feet, cowhocks or a reversion to the Bulldog.

GAIT—Free, smooth, and powerful. When viewed from the side, reach and drive indicate maximum use of the dog's moderate angulation. Back remains level and firm. Coming and going, the dog moves in a straight line. Feet tend to converge under the body, without crossing over, as speed increases. There is no twisting in or out at the joints.

The gait described is the simple, correct movement expected from a working dog with moderate angulation and a compact, nearly square body. Occasionally a Bullmastiff will single track (when all four footprints fall in a single line of travel), but the breed should not generally be expected to do so. The single tracking Bullmastiff should not be confused with a dog that crosses over (when the feet crisscross and toe out) in its movement. This view differs from the current Canadian standard, which asks Bullmastiffs to track in two parallel lines and makes no mention of convergence or single tracking.

Many novice owners mistake speed for good movement. A smooth, moderate trot reveals much more about a dog's soundness and structure than the racing speed often seen in the show ring. As a judge, I am always skeptical when a dog is presented at what I consider excessive speed.

Although good movement should be prized, it should receive no extra recognition if it comes as a benefit of a fault of type. Specifically, a Bullmastiff should get no extra credit for outstanding movement if it lacks the essential compactness and (nearly) square outline, or if it achieves that exceptional movement as a benefit of incorrect type and structure.

TEMPERAMENT—Fearless and confident yet docile. The dog combines the reliability, intelligence, and willingness to please required in a dependable family companion and protector.

Fearless and confident, yet docile. To put it in very simple terms, a Bullmastiff must own the ground it stands on. Docile means to easily teach or manage, not dull or spiritless.

THE BRITISH BULLMASTIFF STANDARD

By Kind Permission of The Kennel Club

GENERAL APPEARANCE—Powerful build, symmetrical, showing great strength, but not cumbersome; sound and active.

CHARACTERISTICS—Powerful, enduring, active and reliable.

TEMPERAMENT—High-spirited, alert and faithful.

HEAD AND SKULL—Skull large and square, viewed from every angle, fair wrinkle when interested, but not when in repose. Circumference of skull may equal height of dog measured at top of shoulder; broad and deep with well filled cheeks. Pronounced stop. Muzzle short; distance from tip of nose to stop approximately one-third of length from tip of nose to centre of occiput, broad under eyes and sustaining nearly same width to end of nose; blunt and cut off square, forming right angle with upper line of face, and at same time proportionate with skull. Underjaw broad to end. Nose broad with widely spreading nostrils; flat, neither pointed nor turned up in profile. Flews not pendulous, never hanging below level of lower jaw.

EYES—Dark or hazel, of medium size, set apart the width of muzzle with furrow between. Light or yellow eyes highly undesirable.

EARS—V-shaped, folded back, set on wide and high, level of occiput giving square appearance to skull, which is most important. Small and deeper in colour than body. Point of ear level with the eye when alert. Rose ears highly undesirable.

MOUTH—Level desired but slightly undershot allowed but not preferred. Canine teeth large and set wide apart, other teeth strong, even and well placed.

NECK—Well arched, moderate length, very muscular and almost equal to skull in circumference.

FOREQUARTERS—Chest, wide and deep, well let down between the forelegs, with deep brisket. Shoulders muscular, sloping and powerful, not overloaded. Forelegs powerful and straight, well boned,

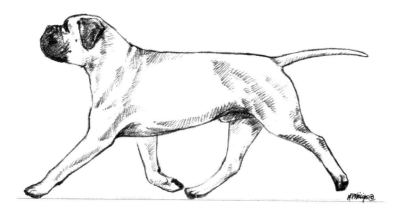

set wide apart, presenting a straight front. Pasterns straight and strong.

BODY—Back short and straight, giving compact carriage, but not so short as to interfere with activity. Roach and sway backs highly undesirable.

HINDQUARTERS—Loins wide and muscular with fair depth of flank. Hindlegs strong and muscular, with well developed second thighs, denoting power and activity, not cumbersome. Hocks moderately bent. Cowhocks highly undesirable.

FEET—Well arched, cat-like, with rounded toes, pads hard. Dark toenails desirable. Splayed feet highly undesirable.

TAIL—Set high, strong at root and tapering, reaching to hocks, carried straight or curved, but not hound-fashion. Crank tails highly undesirable.

GAIT/MOVEMENT—Movement indicates power and sense of purpose. When moving straight neither front nor hindlegs should cross or plait, right front and left rear leg rising and falling at same time. A firm backline unimpaired by powerful thrust from hindlegs denoting a balanced and harmonious movement.

COAT—Short and hard, weather-resistant, lying flat to body. Long, silky or woolly coats highly undesirable.

COLOUR—Any shade of brindle, fawn or red; colour to be pure and clear. A slight white marking on chest permissible. Other white markings undesirable. Black muzzle essential, toning off towards eyes, with dark markings around eyes contributing to expression.

SIZE—Height at shoulder: Dogs: 63.5–68.5 cm (25–27 ins); Bitches: 61–66 cm (24–26 ins). Weight: Dogs: 50–59 kg (110–130 lbs); Bitches: 41–50 kg (90–110 lbs).

FAULTS—Any departure from the foregoing points should be considered a fault and the seriousness with which the fault should be regarded should be in exact proportion to its degree.

NOTE—Male animals should have two apparently normal testicles fully descended into the scrotum.

CANADIAN KENNEL CLUB STANDARD

NOTE: Faults are classified as Serious or Minor, indicated as (S) and (M) respectively. Note the *minor* faults are either points that would not, of themselves, contribute to unsoundness in the dog, or are the result of poor conditioning, which might be controlled, and are not likely to be hereditary.

ORIGIN AND PURPOSE: The Bullmastiff was developed in England by gamekeepers for protection against poachers. The foundation breeding of the modern pure-bred was 60 percent Mastiff and 40 percent Bulldog. It is a guard and companion dog, and should be loyal, obedient, and thus suitable for training.

GENERAL APPEARANCE: The Bullmastiff is a powerfully built, symmetrical dog, showing great strength and activity, but not cumbersome; upstanding and compact in appearance, with breadth and depth of skull and body, the latter set on strong, sturdy, well-boned legs. The height, measured vertically from the ground to the highest point of the withers, should nearly equal the length measured horizontally from the forechest to the rear part of the upper thigh, and should slightly exceed the height at the hips. Bitches are feminine in appearance, of somewhat lighter bone structure than the male, but should still convey strength. Faults: (S) Lack of balance. Poor or light bone structure. (M) Lack of muscular development. Ranginess.

TEMPERAMENT: The Bullmastiff should be bold, fearless and courageous, a dependable guard dog; alert and intelligent. Faults: (S) Viciousness. Shyness. (Such dogs should not be used for breeding.) (M) Apathy and sluggishness.

SIZE: Height at the highest point of the withers—Dogs, 25–27 inches (63–69 cm); Bitches, 24–26 inches (61–66 cm). Weight—Dogs, 110–130 lb. (50–59 kg); Bitches 100–120 lb. (45–55 kg). It is important that weight be in proportion to height and bone structure, to ensure balance. Faults: (S) Over maximum height. Under minimum height. (M) Over maximum weight. Under minimum weight.

COAT AND COLOUR: Coat short and dense, giving good weather protection. Faults: (S) Long, soft coat. (M) "Staring" coat, which means poor condition. Colour: any shade of red, fawn or brindle, but the colour to be pure and clear. A small white marking on the chest permissible but not desirable. Faults: (S) White markings other than on the chest. (M) Black shading on body, legs or tail (of reds or fawns).

HEAD: The *skull* should be large, equal in breadth, length and depth, with a fair amount of wrinkle when the dog is interested; well-developed cheeks. The skull in circumference may measure the height of the dog. Forehead flat, with a furrow between the eyes. Stop definite. Faults: (S) Narrow skull. Shallow skull. (M) Domed forehead. Insufficient stop.

The *muzzle* should be short, broad and deep, in the same proportion as the skull. The distance from the tip of the nose to the stop should not exceed one-third of the length from the tip of the nose to the centre of the occiput. Broad under the eyes and nearly parallel in width to the end of the nose; blunt and cut off square, appearing in profile in a plane parallel in the line of the skull. A black mask is *essential*. The *nose* should be black, flat, and broad with widely spreading nostrils when viewed from the front. Flews not too pendulous. The lower jaw broad. Faults: (S) Muzzle too long, too narrow, pointed or lacking in depth. Muzzle too short; nostrils set on top; nose pointed, upturned or laid back; lower jaw narrow. (M) Lack of wrinkle; flews too pendulous.

Teeth preferably level bite or slightly undershot. Canine teeth large and set wide apart; other teeth strong, even and well placed. Faults: (S) Teeth overshot. Teeth more than one-quarter inch (6 cm) undershot. Wry mouth. (M) Irregular or poorly placed teeth. Small teeth.

Eyes dark or hazel, and of medium size; set apart the width of the muzzle. Faults: (M) Light eyes. Eyes too close together, too large, too small.

"High-spirited, alert and faithful." This is Ch. Bastion's
Celebration Time.

Ears V-shaped and carried close to the cheeks; set on wide and high, level with the occiput, giving a square appearance to the skull which is most important. They should be darker in colour than the body, and the point of the ear, when alert, should be level with the eye. Faults: (S) Rose ears. (M) Ears too long or too short. Lack of darker colour.

NECK: Well arched of moderate length, very muscular, and almost equal in circumference to the skull. Faults: (S) Neck too short; too long. Neck weak and scrawny.

FOREQUARTERS: Proper angulation and proportionate bone lengths of the forequarters are very important. The shoulder bone should slope forward and downward from the withers at an angle of 45 degrees from the vertical. The humerus (upper arm) should form a right angle with the shoulder bone, 45 degrees from the vertical. The shoulder bone and humerus should be approximately equal in length. The length of the foreleg from the ground to the elbow should be a little more than half the distance from the ground to the withers, approximately 52 percent. The shoulders and upper arms should be muscular and powerful, but not overloaded. Forelegs powerful, with round heavy bone, vertical and parallel to each other, set well apart; elbows set close to the body. Pasterns straight and strong. Feet of medium size, not turning in or out, with rounded toes, well arched. Pads thick and tough. Nails black. Faults: (S) Lack of proportion in bone. Shoulder too steep. Shoulders overloaded. Elbows turned in or out. Lack of bone in forelegs. Forelegs bowed. Weak pasterns. Splay feet. (M) Feet turned in or out. White nails.

BODY AND TAIL: Body compact. Chest wide and deep, with ribs well sprung and well set down between the forelegs. Back short and level. Loins wide, muscular; croup slightly arched, with fair depth of flank. Faults: (S) Body too long. Shallow chest. Lack of ribspring. Sway back. Roach back. Tip of hip bone higher than withers. (M) Too much tuck-up.

Tail set on high, strong at the root and tapering to the hocks. It may be carried straight or curved. Faults: (S) Screw tail. Crank tail. Tail set too low. (M) Tail carried hound fashion. Too long. Too short. Too heavily coated.

HINDQUARTERS: It is important that structure, angulation, and proportionate bone lengths of the hindquarters be in balance with the forequarters. The pelvis (hip bone) should slope backward and downward from the spine at an angle of 30 degrees. The femur (upper thigh bone) should form a right angle with the pelvis. The lower thigh bone (stifle) should set at an angle of 45 degrees to the vertical. The pelvis and femur should be approximately equal in length. The ratio of the lengths of the femur, to the tibia/fibula, to the hocks should be approximately as 4:5:3. The length of the lower leg, from the ground to the hock joint, should be a little less than 30 percent of the distance from the ground to the top of the hip bones. The lower leg should be vertical to the ground. The hips should be broad, in balance with shoulders and rib cage. Hind legs strong and muscular, with well developed second thighs, denoting power and activity, but not cumbersome, set parallel to each other and well apart, in balance with forelegs and body. Feet as in forequarters. Faults: (S) Lack of proportion in bone. Poor angulation at hip bone. Narrow hip structure. Stifle too straight or over-angulated. Cow hocks. Bowed hind legs. Splay feet. (M) Feet turned in or out. White nails.

GAIT: The gait should be free, balanced and vigorous. When viewed from the side the dog should have good reach in the forequarters and good driving power in the hindquarters. The back should be level and firm, indicating good transmission from rear to front. When viewed from the front (coming toward) or from the rear (going away), at a moderate pace, the dog shall track in two parallel, neither too close together nor too far apart, so placed as to give a strong well-balanced movement. The toes (fore and hind) should point straight ahead.

DIRECTIONS TO EXHIBITORS AND JUDGES: The dog should be moved in the ring at a sufficient speed to show fluidity of movement, and not at a slow walk. Faults: (S) Rolling, paddling, or weaving when gaited. Any crossing movement, either front or rear. Stilted and restricted movement. (Dogs with structural weakness as evidenced by poor movement should not be used for breeding.)

DISQUALIFICATIONS: Liver mask. No mask. Yellow eyes.

(Gail Painter)

CHAPTER 4

Finding the Right Dog

The best place to buy a Bullmastiff is from a responsible breeder with a reputation for having healthy dogs with good temperament. Breeders spend years concentrating on producing mentally and physically sound dogs. Their selective breeding programs are aimed at maintaining the virtues of the breed and eliminating genetic flaws. Responsible breeders care about every puppy they produce for the lifetime of the dog, and will work with you to make the right match and build the right relationship with your dog.

FINDING A BREEDER

So where does an interested person begin to search for that Bullmastiff puppy from a respectable breeder? Unless you know people who own Bullmastiffs or who show dogs of other breeds, this can sometimes be difficult. This is not a common breed, and puppies may not be available where you live.

If you live in the United States, you can call or write to the American Kennel Club and ask for the address and phone number of the secretary of the American Bullmastiff Association and the ABA information chairman. When you call the club officials, ask for a list of breeders and if there are any upcoming dog shows in the area where you can go see the dogs and meet some Bullmastiff owners and breeders.

If you live in Britain or Canada, you can write to the KC or the CKC for the same information. The addresses of all these organizations are in Appendix F.

Do remember that the American Kennel Club (and its international counterparts) is primarily a registry for purebred dogs. It certifies that the dog is purebred and from particular parentage. It is not a seal

A good Bullmastiff breeder cares about maintaining the virtues of the breed. Left is Ch. Blazin's Blue Max, an excellent Bullmastiff dog, and right is Ch. Blackslate's Spirit of Boston, an excellent Bullmastiff bitch.

of approval nor an indication of quality for an individual puppy or dog.

Another place to look for breeders is in the AKC's monthly magazine, *AKC Gazette,* which is accompanied by a supplement called *Events Calendar.* These periodicals can be found in many public libraries across the United States. The *Gazette* contains interesting articles about purebred dogs, columns about individual breeds and advertisements from dog breeders, and *Events Calendar* lists all the championship-level AKC dog shows around the country for the upcoming months.

There are other commercial dog magazines available on the newsstand. Some offer a list of shows and events, as well as featured and classified ads for dogs. The key word to remember is that these are *commercial* enterprises with little control or knowledge of their individual advertisers. Some reputable breeders and clubs may advertise in such magazines, but so do the commercial dog breeders and large puppy breeding facilities. Ask for references and check information carefully when dealing with magazine or newspaper ads.

Make sure you check references very carefully. I once had the strange experience of being called by a prospective Bullmastiff buyer who had been told by a puppy dealer that he sold one of his pups "to the president of the American Bullmastiff Association"—me. I assured the man that I had neither purchased a pup from that person nor had I any knowledge of that individual or kennel. If he had not checked, he would have been seriously misled.

When dealing with strangers without personal recommendations and references, all we can say is *buyer beware*. There are many caring, committed breeders selling dogs—enough that you will be able to find one.

It is often far better to attend a dog show to meet contented owners, and to get referrals and recommendations from the people who are there with their dogs. Most will be glad to tell you about puppies they might have available, or about a breeding that has been done, or one that is planned. Those who are not breeders themselves can refer you to the people who sold them their Bullmastiff, or may be able to recommend a friend or acquaintance with a litter.

At a show, always buy the show catalog. In addition to the name of each entry, it contains the name and address of each owner, as well as the age, parentage and breeders of every dog in the show. Mark down the winners in each class and also note the dogs you found to be particularly interesting. If it's possible, go to several shows to watch the Bullmastiffs. Eventually a pattern will emerge from your notations about the dogs and the winners, and you will have a clearer picture of the dog you want and the breeders you want to contact. Going to shows also affords an excellent opportunity to see firsthand if the sport of dog showing might be fun for you.

Even if you are unable to speak to an individual at the show itself, the catalog makes it possible to contact the owner or breeder of the dogs you like at a later date. At larger shows, it also gives you an opportunity to observe the Bullmastiffs from various lines in the ring together, to compare them

Your dog should look alert while still nicely stacking in the ring. This is Ch. Blackslate's Boston Brahmin.

and to decide which dogs are more appealing to you personally. When looking for a potential show or breeding-quality Bullmastiff, it is essential to remember that what you like is always secondary to what is correct in the written standard for the breed.

SELECTING A BREEDER

Give some very serious attention to the people who offer to sell you a Bullmastiff, regardless of whether they were contacted in response to a referral, an ad or a meeting at a dog show. If possible, choose a conscientious and knowledgeable breeder with a reputation for producing both winning show dogs and loving pets.

Whether the puppy you are inquiring about is the breeder's first effort, or a litter from a person with 20 years' experience, they should all uniformly share a concern for the breed and for the

This Australian puppy, Bullmaster Storm Cloud, shows good type for his age.

future well-being of their puppies. Don't be surprised if you are screened almost as thoroughly as if you were applying to adopt a human child. Usually this type of cautious and caring breeder will remain a resource for helpful advice, genuine concern and answers to the many questions that will arise during the life of the dog.

Choose people who are knowledgeable about the breed standard, the background and history of the breed; who answer your questions helpfully and honestly; and who are willing to give you the names of their veterinarian and some of their earlier puppy buyers for references. Ask questions about their experience in the breed, why they chose Bullmastiffs, and why they are breeding dogs. Find out what health screening they do with

their dogs, and any particular health problems or strengths present in their bloodline.

Ask if they own or keep other breeds of dogs, and if so, whether they are involved in breeding (or showing) them, too. Many reputable Bullmastiff breeders have a dog or two of another breed, but kennels that frequently produce a variety of puppies to sell to pet homes are generally considered to be commercial breeding establishments, and should be avoided. These commercial breeders derive a significant portion of their income from the business of raising dogs, and are driven by profit rather than a serious commitment to Bullmastiffs. They do not generally belong to the associations and clubs dedicated to the preservation and protection of the breed, often follow no code of ethics, frequently offer wonderful-sounding but worthless guarantees, and can sometimes be identified by advertisements that tout USDA inspection or approval, all major credit cards, shipping anywhere and many champion bloodlines available.

WHAT TO LOOK FOR IN A PUPPY

Ideally, it is best to visit a breeder's home or kennel to see the puppies in their natural surroundings and to see the mother and any other related dogs living there. Some breeders do not allow visits until after the pups have had their first inoculations. However, a buyer should always expect to be permitted to inspect the puppies and the home conditions at some time before they actually buy a dog. When you visit the home or kennel, it should be a healthy environment with clean, well-cared-for dogs and pups.

Choose people who are knowledgeable about the breed and have had success in their breeding and showing program.

Many breeders encourage visitors beginning when the pups are approximately six weeks old. If there are children in your family, take them with you to see the litter but caution them in advance about proper behavior with small puppies and adult dogs. Most breeders are hesitant to sell a puppy to a household with children who treat dogs roughly or who are themselves wild and poorly behaved.

A puppy between six and eight weeks of age should be sturdy, steady on its legs, curious and active. It should have the look of a Bullmastiff in miniature, with a solid, compact body, firm back and topline, good bone on its straight legs and angulation that is equally balanced front and rear. A good bite should be broad and, at this young age, may be either scissors or level. The lower jaw usually continues to lengthen as the Bullmastiff matures, so a distinctly under-shot puppy (where the lower jaw extends farther than the upper) at six weeks might show its bottom teeth as an adult.

The head should show evidence of the wrinkle pattern that the dog will have as an adult. Some bloodlines are heavily wrinkled as small puppies but tend to smooth out as they mature. In other lines the opposite may be true. This is a question that should be asked of the breeder, and perhaps photos of their dogs as pups and again at adulthood can be studied for reference.

The skull and muzzle should be broad and deep, giving a square impression to the head. You should be able to feel a very slight indentation at the stop, where the muzzle joins the skull. Neither the muzzle nor the head should appreciably taper or narrow. The look should be square, and that also means the planes of the head, muzzle and underjaw should be approximately parallel when looking at a puppy from the side.

The eyes of a young puppy can sometimes have a slight smoky gray color, which normally goes away, but the darker the eyes, the less risk of light eyes in the adult. They should always be clear and bright, with no weeping or evidence of chronic tears.

Look for large, well-opened nostrils for ease in breathing. The ears should be moderate in size, not large, and they should be set well up on the head rather than hanging out from the sides. Masks can

When you visit a kennel, you should see healthy, well-cared-for pups.
(Amy Hayward)

A basket of happy puppies, one fawn, one red fawn and one brindle.
(Dr. David Hopps)

vary in size and shape, but the muzzle should always be black and there should be black around the eyes.

Color is a difficult thing to predict in the six- to eight-week-old puppy. The best place to check for coat color is the top of the head around the occipital bone. If there is a faint but definite cast of red at this age, and if either of the parents are red or red fawn, the puppy will likely grow up to be a red or red fawn dog. The shade will normally be much darker at maturity than is evidenced by the pup's head color.

Some puppies are born with a heavy, dark overlay on the back and chest. Occasionally they might have black on the legs and feet as well. Another variation is a puppy with a normal clear coat on the top but a significantly lighter underside, ranging all the way to a nearly white or pale cream color. Typically, many types of puppy shading will fade away with age, but it is best to note whether the parents or any close relatives retained that same coloration. This can be an indication of what to expect once the puppy reaches adulthood. While odd coloration and markings do not significantly affect the value of the puppy as a pet and companion, they can be a major hindrance in the show ring or in a breeding program.

White markings on a small puppy may also diminish with time and growth,

A puppy should look like a Bullmastiff in miniature. (Amy Hayward)

especially at the tips of the toes. However, for a show prospect, choose the pup of the best overall quality who possesses the least white and the fewest cosmetic faults.

PET OR SHOW DOG?

It is fairly common for an experienced breeder to grade the litter and then to place the puppies according to the needs and wishes of the buyer. An inexperienced or first-time Bullmastiff buyer would probably do best by explaining carefully and truthfully exactly what characteristics are most important to them, and what they want to do with the dog, and then let the breeder's experience guide their choice. A "pick of the litter" puppy can vary from the best in the litter to the very least specimen. It all depends on the expertise of the person who is doing the picking and on what the buyer is looking for.

When selecting a puppy as a household pet and companion, the finer details of the standard will not be of as great a significance as they are to the person looking for a pup that may someday be shown or bred. Consider what characteristics are most important to you, and do not be overly concerned with the other non-structural defects or cosmetic faults that do not affect the dog's health and well-being. Short or crooked tails, slighter masks, white toes, color variations, longer muzzles, smaller size or lighter bone may cause a puppy to be automatically considered pet quality by the breeder. But those pets can still make top-quality companions. If an available pet puppy has any of these faults and if they are not on your list of personal requirements and preferences, you may have found the puppy for you. Often the obvious pets in a litter are the first ones promised to buyers.

The time to consider whether you are interested in showing or breeding your Bullmastiff is before you make the purchase. Show quality indicates more than just a higher price for a puppy. It usually means the breeder believes a particular pup appears to closely fit the standard, and has some potential to win in the show ring based on its qualities and the absence of major faults.

When you are looking at the conformation of a puppy, remember that once a pup passes nine or 10 weeks of age, the entire appearance often changes. Pups may move into a less compact, or gangly stage, and may no longer have that complete, adult-in-miniature look about them. Heads look less blocky. Overall they become more difficult to physically evaluate, but are still of an excellent age to go to a new home. Breeders sometimes refer to this period as "the puppy uglies." Although it varies from line to line, it can often last until the dog nears its first birthday and causes much hand wringing and worry both for experts and novice owners.

This bitch puppy is five weeks old and a future champion.

TEMPERAMENT TESTING

Puppy aptitude tests, puppy personality profiles and temperament testing are all names for basically similar sets of exercises that some breeders use to further evaluate their pups for proper placement or to help search for particular skills and abilities in the dogs they wish to keep. These tests involve evaluating a puppy in a new environment at approximately seven weeks of age to check for its sensitivity to sound, touch, confinement and immobilization, and its willingness to follow, come and retrieve. They also address such concerns as prey drive, biting instinct and the pup's willingness and ability to forgive and to reconcile to the tester after completing an exercise that it did not particularly like.

When correctly administered, the results of these tests can be valuable in recognizing behavior and personality traits that may be encouraged or discouraged by socialization and training. For example, a breeder would not likely wish to place a pup that is very pain- or sound-sensitive in a family with toddlers or noisy young children, while a person hoping to compete in the obedience ring would be encouraged to accept the outgoing puppy that shows the strongest desire to retrieve a tossed paper ball or to naturally come or follow close to the tester.

Each test method has a system of scoring each exercise, and those scores and the total score, it is hoped, equate to predictions of potential, personality or innate instinct. If testing and evaluation are offered when you shop for your puppy, ask the breeder to explain the method to you and the

After about 10 weeks, pups are more difficult to evaluate. The one on the left is three months old and the one on the right is five months old.

significance of the scoring for the puppies under consideration.

In some cases, potential puppy buyers may attend the test as quiet observers. When I lived in a large home in Philadelphia, the living room with its adjoining, sweeping staircase offered a perfect vantage point for puppy buyers to sit out of the pup's line of vision and watch the proceedings. The puppy buyers would be invited to come on the pups' 49th day to observe the temperament tests. Each could hold a score sheet and write down the numbers interpreted by the tester for the puppy they were considering.

THE LONG-DISTANCE PUPPY

Although an individual seeking a family pet and companion will usually try to buy a Bullmastiff as close to home as possible, many of the people looking for show prospects and some of those seeking pets of a particular sex, color, age or line may find they need to go farther afield in their search for the right puppy and a breeder with whom they feel comfortable. Photographs, pedigrees, telephone calls, e-mail and the easy availability of videotapes of the parents and the litter make buying a Bullmastiff puppy from a long distance away a more frequent and suitable option.

The major drawbacks are the inability to visit the puppy and the kennel before the purchase, and the necessity of either having to ship the puppy or to travel a great distance to pick it up. And, unless otherwise agreed in advance, the costs and charges for shipping or transporting the puppy are the responsibility of the buyer.

Some breeders will accommodate a buyer by arranging to meet at a convenient point halfway between their locations. It may also be possible for the puppy to be delivered by a third party who might be traveling to a dog show or on a vacation.

If the puppy is being shipped by air, every effort should be made to ensure its comfort and well-being by using nonstop or direct flights on an airline that offers priority or counter-to-counter parcel service for small animals. This differs from regular cargo shipping in that the puppy does not have to arrive at the airport quite so early and is handled in the same manner as the pets traveling with their owners as excess baggage. For a young

Bullmastiff puppy, it is well worth the small extra cost when this option is available.

By planning far ahead, it is also sometimes possible for a puppy buyer to secure a round-trip ticket at a reduced or sale fare that only slightly exceeds the regular shipping costs for the dog alone. This somewhat more costly endeavor allows the buyer the opportunity to visit the kennel and to view the entire litter. Some airlines allow a small animal to ride in an approved container in the passenger cabin. However, only the very smallest and youngest of Bullmastiff pups can fit into an under-seat container or a canvas pet carrier or shoulder bag approved for in-cabin flight.

SALES CONTRACTS, AGREEMENTS AND PAPERS

The price of a Bullmastiff puppy varies considerably from breeder to breeder as well as between geographical regions and among different countries. Some of the top breeders charge less for their puppies than many pet shops. The time to compare prices and ask questions about terms or shipping costs is before committing to buy a Bullmastiff.

It is common for a Bullmastiff breeder to ask for a modest deposit on a puppy once a litter is safely whelped and it is apparent that a puppy is actually available of the sex and requirements you stated. At times a deposit must be paid before the pups are old enough to safely have outside visitors, particularly if the breeder has many people on his or her waiting list. This is necessary to ensure that all the puppies that have been reserved are definitely wanted. A litter is frequently advertised

months in advance, so a breeder believing all of his litter is sold can be at a great disadvantage if the sales are not actually finalized. Although such a deposit is not unreasonable after an anticipated litter actually arrives, unless you personally know the breeders involved, it is prudent to avoid paying a down payment on any litter before puppies are whelped. Pay these deposits by check, or be sure to receive a receipt with an explanation of the terms of the payment. Often a deposit is non-refundable unless a puppy becomes unavailable due to its death or a permanent infirmity.

Just as buyers want to be sure they are dealing with an ethical person when purchasing a puppy, breeders also want to be sure they've found the best possible home for each pup. This can give rise to all sorts of conditions, contracts and agreements relating to a sale. These may range from simple statements that the dog is to be returned to the breeder if the buyers can no longer keep it, to complex ownership, breeding and showing contracts popular with some breeders.

Ask to see a copy or outline of any detailed contract or agreement before the date of sale (and before you pay a non-refundable deposit), to avoid any last-minute surprises. It is very hard to refuse to sign a contract once the puppy is snuggling in your arms or blissfully licking your hands. Read and completely understand what is being required of both parties in all contracts. If the contract seems restrictive or complex, if it is extremely long and involved, or if it requires co-ownership with shared breeding and showing, it may be wise to have a lawyer check the document before you sign. Also, carefully review all health certifications, guarantees and warranties offered by the breeder, and ask to clarify or amend any areas of concern in writing. Be sure that all alterations or corrections are initialed and dated by all the parties involved in the sale.

Pet puppies are usually sold outright, but often with some sort of spay-neuter contract to ensure that the dog is not to be bred. More and more reputable breeders are becoming concerned with the issues of canine overpopulation and the sad effects of the ever-increasing numbers of Bullmastiffs in need of rescue. In the United States, the pet-quality puppy is likely to be sold with AKC Limited Registration papers. This is a choice the breeder makes when first transferring ownership. A Limited Registration means the animal is purebred, has a certifiable pedigree, but is not sold for breeding or for conformation showing purposes. These dogs may participate in performance events such as Obedience, Tracking and Agility. However, the AKC does not permit regular showing and will not register any offspring from that dog. To the average pet buyer uninterested in breeding or showing, Limited Registration should be of absolutely no concern or consequence.

Because puppies do change their appearance quite a bit as they mature, a breeder can rescind Limited Registration by completing a form and filing it with the AKC.

Whether the puppy is purely a pet or is a show ring hopeful, the breeder should supply each buyer of a purebred Bullmastiff with a three- to five-generation pedigree and the official registration papers, if they have arrived from the AKC. (Unless you know the breeder, or they come very highly recommended, it is usually not a good idea to buy a dog with a promise of papers to come later.) A Bill of Sale should also be prepared with the following information:

- The date of sale
- The date of birth
- The sex, color and markings of the puppy
- Permanent identification, such as tattoos or microchips
- The names and registration numbers of the sire and dam
- The names of the breeders and the buyers
- The complete addresses and telephone numbers of all parties
- Any conditions to the sale, such as Limited Registration
- The dated signatures of the buyers and the sellers

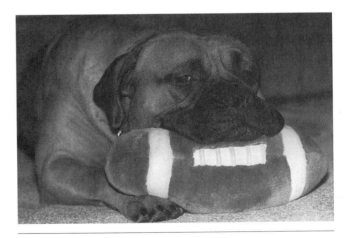

Every dog deserves a chance to be somebody's pet. (Gail Painter)

CONSIDERING AN OLDER DOG

For some individuals, an adult Bullmastiff can be a better choice than buying a young puppy. Some of these dogs are available because of an unexpected transfer, a divorce, changes in circumstances, or an allergy to dogs. Occasionally a breeder will also have a dog that was returned, was not quite what they had hoped for in the show ring, or perhaps is a retired Champion who did not fit into their breeding program for one reason or another. Sometimes people simply find themselves with too many Bullmastiffs to be able to give them all the individual attention they deserve, and decide to secure a better home for one or more dogs.

Whatever the reason, there can be definite advantages to acquiring an adult Bullmastiff. The most obvious point is that the dog is mature and a buyer knows exactly what he or she is getting in terms of size, conformation and soundness. The dog is usually housebroken and is past the puppy chewing stage. Some may have received basic obedience training or have been successfully raised with other small pets or children.

In many cases the adult Bullmastiff comes with a full history and has developed its own temperament and personality traits. It is quicker and easier to evaluate a grown dog's behavior, preferences and dislikes. Others may have been abandoned, neglected or abused, and are deeply grateful for a new home with loving owners.

One of the main concerns with buying or adopting an older dog is whether the animal will adjust to its new home. People tend to romanticize their dogs and believe that their pet could not be

A puppy is right for some people, but an adult is the ideal choice for others.

happy without them. Some dogs do grieve at the loss of an owner or a canine companion, but they are the exception. The fact is that when adult dogs go to a new home where they receive attention, affection and good care, they normally settle into the household after a transition period of approximately three to four weeks. Retired show dogs can be particularly adaptable, because they are accustomed to traveling and spending time away from home.

As a person who has taken in adult dogs off and on for most of my life, I can state that the first three to four weeks can be a time of trial and adjustment for both the dog and new owner.

Perseverance is sometimes necessary to stick it out for the full transition period, but almost invariably the day finally comes when all the stress suddenly disappears and dog and person come to recognize the fact that they belong together.

THE RESCUE DOG

There is a special place in heaven for the people who look after the lost, abandoned and abused Bullmastiffs of the world. Many of these dedicated souls also show and breed dogs, but feel a special responsibility to help the breed that gives them so much enjoyment and pleasure. Some are simply dog lovers who detest suffering in any form. They often travel long distances and spend their own funds to secure a Bullmastiff in need. They foster the dogs to evaluate health and temperament, and eventually give them up to good permanent homes.

Rescue dogs come from various sources. A small percentage are given up by the owners to an organized rescue program, such as American Bullmastiff Association Rescue, and the other rescue schemes sponsored by clubs and individuals in various countries. Some dogs are strays found wandering the streets, some are from shelters, and some

The day will come when your dog realizes you belong together. (Dominique DeVito)

have been saved from abuse and neglect.

In years past it was almost unheard of for a Bullmastiff to end up in an animal shelter. Unfortunately, it has become increasingly common in the past decade, both in the United States and abroad. A glance at the comparative registration statistics in Appendix A will suggest that the recent increase of Bullmastiffs in need of rescue might only be the beginning of even worse problems to come.

Both the American Bullmastiff Association and the Canadian Bullmastiff fanciers have Web sites showing photos of rescued Bullmastiffs that are available for adoption. The American Bullmastiff Rescue Web page is http://www.akc.org/clubs/aba/index.html, and the Canadian rescue page is http://www.geocities.com/athens/1300/rescue.html. You can also contact your local Bullmastiff club, the AKC or the kennel club of your country for assistance in finding rescue organizations.

These dogs deserve a new chance at life. They can make excellent companions and they can guard a home and family as well as the most high-priced show dog. Please think of them, too, when you are considering adding a Bullmastiff to your family.

CHAPTER 5

Raising a Bullmastiff

The day you bring home a new dog can be one of the most exciting, memorable days of your life. If you reserved a puppy in advance from a planned litter, you may have waited many months, or even a year, for your pet. When the day finally arrives, make sure you're ready.

PREPARING FOR THE NEW ARRIVAL

Every new Bullmastiff owner needs to make a list of supplies and equipment, find the proper brand of dog food recommended by the breeder, decide on a veterinarian, read some puppy rearing and training books (such as *The Howell Book of Puppy Raising* by Charlotte Schwartz), and locate an appropriate training school for the expected arrival well before the dog arrives. These things need to be done in advance to ensure a smooth transition for both the dog and the proud new family. Basic equipment for the anticipated arrival should include:

- A crate of sufficient size for a fast-growing dog (this simplifies housetraining).

- Bedding that can be easily washed and dried (avoid comforters and quilts stuffed with polyester or similar fine fibers, which can be ingested and cause intestinal blockage).

- An adjustable flat collar and a four- to six-foot leather or cotton-webbing leash (no choke collars or chains for the young puppy).

This is Ch. Ladybug Lady Caitlin, TD, the winningest bitch in the breed, at 10 weeks old. Let's watch her grow up.

- Two stainless steel, ceramic or glass dog bowls (no plastic).

- Grooming tools: a soft bristle brush or hound's glove, a fine-toothed flea comb, a rubber curry comb, a metal slicker brush, a shedding blade (for older dogs) and nail clippers.

- Cleaning supplies for accidents on the floor or carpet, including odor removers such as Nature's Miracle or Odor Ban.

- Paper towels and a supply of old but clean rags.

- Toys: soft fleece or furry toys, a medium ball and chew toys of various kinds.

HOMECOMING

Try to plan your new dog's homecoming so it coincides with the beginning of a weekend, a holiday or time off from your normal work or travel schedule. Bringing a new puppy or pet home is exciting, and children will want to play with it. Friends and neighbors will want to stop in to see the Bullmastiff puppy. Existing pets will be curious and sometimes resentful, and puppies must be carefully introduced into the household to prevent jealousy on the part of the resident adult dogs.

It's important to remember that a young puppy is still an infant and might find leaving its littermates and birthplace to be a tiring or traumatic event. Try to keep the noise and confusion to a minimum. Begin by taking the puppy to the place outside where you want it to eliminate. Once it relieves itself, bring it into the house for a full introduction to its new family and home. Offer some water and show the dog where the water bowl is to be kept. However, do not offer food unless it is the regularly scheduled time for a meal. Show the dog its crate and bed area, and place a small treat or biscuit inside for it to discover.

Let the puppy explore its surroundings and find some of its new toys, but always keep the dog in sight. Be ever alert for signs that the pup might need to go outside again.

If there are small children in the family, have them sit quietly on the floor when holding the

Caitlin at 16 weeks.

puppy and remind them of the basic ground rules for behavior with dogs. Be watchful that neither child nor puppy hurts each other. Those needle-sharp teeth and untrimmed nails can badly scratch a small youngster. Dropping or an inadvertent step on a foot or tail can injure the young puppy. Child-dog relationships are formed right from the start; the adult owners are responsible for starting them off on the right foot.

After 20 to 40 minutes of play and exploration, the pup should be taken back outside until it relieves itself. Then bring it in, place it in its crate with another tiny treat and a toy such as a knotted cotton rope segment or a furry soft toy, and leave it there for a much-needed nap.

Except for praising good behavior and the regular schedule of out-play-out-sleep, the first day is not for teaching or training. Carefully supervise any contact with existing pets and prevent any unpleasant incidents before they happen.

It has been my experience that most Bullmastiff puppies adapt quickly to their new environment and often will sleep through the night without any crying or fuss, unless they need to go out. There are two main schools of thought about handling cries in the night from a new puppy. Some people think the puppy should be left alone and expected to sleep without any further comfort or assistance from the new owners. Others like to bring the puppy into the bedroom and place the crate or a large box next to their bed where they can dangle a hand down for a reassuring pat from time to time. A happy medium would be to get up if the pup persists in crying for any length of time, and take it outside if that is what's needed. Once assured that the pup is not in distress, new owners should firmly close the door, pull a pillow over their ears and get some sleep. This behavior normally only lasts for a few nights, if handled without undue fuss and attention.

HOUSETRAINING

Bullmastiffs are basically clean dogs and are relatively easy to housetrain with a little persistence. The task is often begun naturally in the first two weeks of life, when the blind, almost helpless pups begin to feel the first urges to eliminate on their

Caitlin at eight months.

own and struggle away from the center of the whelping box to beyond the edge of the bedding to relieve themselves. Housetraining is simply a

reinforcement of that natural tendency to avoid fouling the den by expanding the dog's concept of den to cover the entire house. This means the owners must make a concerted effort to begin the housetraining from the time the pup first arrives. This involves:

- Restricting the pup to a small sleeping area such as a crate.

- Diligently watching the puppy whenever it is playing or at large in the house.

- Taking time for frequent trips outdoors.

- Waiting patiently in any weather until the pup actually succeeds in urinating and/or emptying its bowels.

- Staying up late enough at night and getting up early enough in the morning to avoid accidents in the pup's bed area.

- Lavishing praise and attention every single time the puppy performs when it is taken outdoors.

- Teaching a particular word that the dog will learn to connect with the deed; this word is later used to encourage the dog to go at times it might feel are inopportune.

Ideally, someone will be available the first few weeks to take the puppy out on a regular schedule. These outings should be every few hours, beginning with the dog's first stirrings in the early morning and ending with one last trip outside late at night. It also needs to go out before any freedom or play time in the house, whenever it awakens from an extended nap, after eating a meal and after approximately 15 to 20 minutes of sustained play or excited activity.

The crate or bed area should always contain a clean, soft blanket or other form of bedding that is laundered at least once a week and is checked daily for any odor or slight dampness. The presence of clean, fresh-smelling bedding encourages the dog to prefer cleanliness in its surroundings. Of course, it should be removed immediately if there is any accidental soiling. After cleaning the crate or bed area, make the puppy wait a few minutes in a bare bed before replacing the clean bedding. This is to prevent the dog from confusing the arrival of a fresh blanket with a reward for the original mistake.

Caitlin at two years.

Another factor to consider in housetraining is the dog's own body rhythms. Pay attention to what times of day the puppy most easily complies when you take it out. This will give you a good clue as to how long it takes your puppy to digest its meal. A good rule of thumb is that it generally takes approximately eight hours from meal to output. The more often a pup eats, the more those distinctions tend to overlap and blur. However, at night they still mostly hold true. A pup who has difficulty sleeping through the night without incident is often being fed its last meal too early in the evening. Although a dog being fed at 5 to 6 o'clock in the evening might eliminate during its bedtime walk, the main urge to empty its bowels will often occur sometime after 1 or 2 o'clock in the morning. Getting up to attend to the whining pup avoids accidents and unnecessary cleanup, but it does nothing to train the young Bullmastiff to sleep quietly through the night. Switching to a 9 or 10 o'clock evening meal might more easily solve the problem, and allow both dog and master to sleep until a more civilized hour after dawn.

Caitlin at seven years.

Housetraining an acquired adult Bullmastiff is normally no more difficult than starting with a young puppy. It involves the same basic methods and procedures used with a puppy. While the dog may lack the house and den concept, the older dog does have an advantage in that its digestive system is mature and far more predictable, requiring fewer trips outside.

There are really three parts to successful housetraining: The first is to firmly establish the concept in the dog's mind that cleanliness is a desirable virtue best accomplished by going outdoors or using a spot designated by the master; the second is to expand the dog's ingrained concept of den to the owner's entire home; the third is to adjust human schedules and the natural body rhythm of the dog so that they work together positively toward success.

BASIC TRAINING FOR YOUR BULLMASTIFF

Bullmastiffs are what may generously be termed a strong-willed breed. They are also very intelligent and unbelievably inventive and persistent in getting their own way. What is "cute" misbehavior in a 30-pound puppy is definitely not so enchanting in an adult weighing 100 pounds or more. The breed was designed as a working companion and guard to humans. Traits of protectiveness, confidence, loyalty, steadiness, discrimination, independence and focused aggression are still in the breed today. In general, that means the Bullmastiff will allow its owners to be in charge but will typically be ever ready to take control whenever it perceives the need (true or not).

As with housetraining, it is best to start right from the beginning to mold the dog into what you deem to be proper and acceptable behavior. The keys to successful training are clarity, consistency, firmness and reward. The Bullmastiff must clearly understand what is wanted of it. A puppy is not born with a full vocabulary, so it makes sense to teach one command at a time. For instance, once it has fully mastered the sit, then go on to the next command.

You must be consistent in what and how you ask the dog to perform. When you are certain the dog understands what you want, the dog must execute the command every time you ask. It must understand the meaning of the word "no," and you have to be willing to enforce any breach of good behavior.

A short training session every day or at set intervals during the week is preferable to long, intense drills. Bullmastiffs learn quickly, but they will also quickly lose interest in repeating the same exercise time after time. They must be motivated to want to please you and to perform and behave in a certain manner. While some breeds are excited by a pat on the head, a tossed ball, a tug on a towel or a tussle with a toy furry rat, most Bullmastiffs would rather work for pay. That means rewarding them constantly while learning and later rewarding them frequently just to remind them that you still fully appreciate the "good dog." Until fairly recently, there was a stigma attached to using any form of food treats for motivation and

Caitlin at nine years old.

rewards. This is not true now, so feel free to reward your Bullmastiff in the way that gets the best results.

It has been shown that puppies that are socialized, trained and taught skills in the first four months of life are better able to learn and interact all their lives. Puppy kindergarten or preschool might seem like a waste of time and money, but in a dominant, sometimes dog-aggressive breed like the Bullmastiff, it can have tremendous value as the dog matures. The owner learns to control and teach the puppy in a non-punitive manner, while in the midst of all sorts of distractions. The puppy learns not only a few rudimentary commands, but also discovers that interaction with other dogs can be a pleasant and interesting experience.

As a rule, the adult Bullmastiff is not a reliably sociable animal with strange canines, and such early socializing may mean the difference between

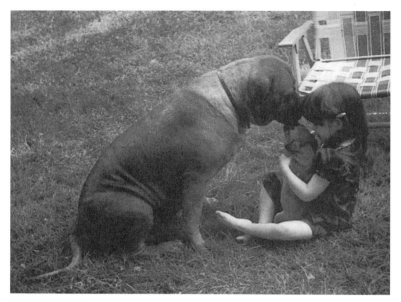

You are responsible for making sure your children and your puppy start off right.

a dog you can enjoy taking out in public or to a show, and a canine Atilla the Hun who cannot seem to resist threatening every other dog in sight. Puppy classes can help to ease that aggressive tendency later on, and in some cases, those puppy friendships allow lifelong preferences or tolerances for certain other breeds. My very first Bullmastiff met a Great Dane bitch at nine weeks of age in kindergarten and became friends. Even at eight or nine years old, she would still perk up and get excited at the sight of an approaching Dane.

A Bullmastiff can learn a surprisingly large vocabulary. All dogs should learn to come, sit, down and stay, and to walk on a leash without dragging the owner all over the place. Dogs should

also comprehend what "no" or "stop" means. Mastering these simple commands won't earn your Bullmastiff an Obedience title, but they will make living with it a much more pleasant experience for both dog and family.

BULLMASTIFFS AND CHILDREN

Because I have both raised a large family and bred Bullmastiffs for many years, I frequently am asked whether this is a good breed for a family with children. Frankly, if I had not found that to be generally true, I would not still own and breed them. As with any large dog, a certain amount of care and caution should be exercised, but overall the Bullmastiff's stability, discrimination and calm personality make it a good choice for families wishing to have a large, protective dog.

Among guard-type breeds, the Bullmastiff's natural tendency to knock down their victims, rather than to bite and slash at first provocation, gives an added measure of safety where children are concerned. The breed's stoic ability to withstand discomfort allows it to be patient with clumsy toddlers who accidentally tread on toes or tails and to accept the attentions of persistent children who interrupt meals or nap times. Because the breed is rarely neurotic or extremely jealous, adults who plan to add a baby to the family can normally expect the Bullmastiff to accept and to become rather fond of the new arrival.

Parents bear the responsibility of selecting a puppy or adult dog that is compatible with the family lifestyle, and of socializing and training both the dog and the children to encourage mutual respect and affection. When selecting a puppy, avoid the dominant and more excitable or active ones in the litter. Test for pain sensitivity by exerting increasing pressure on the webbing between the toes. The longer it takes the pup to register discomfort, the better. An adult dog of placid disposition in need of a new home might be an excellent choice for a family, and bringing home an adult dog bypasses housetraining and the other negative aspects of puppy rearing.

There is a difference between a Bullmastiff as a family dog and one that is to belong to a certain child. Because dogs are pack animals, the Bullmastiff will naturally attempt to place itself as high in the household social order as possible. Aside from any order of dominance among the other pets, the Bullmastiff usually obeys and looks up to the adults in the household, and tends to benevolently consider the children as charges entrusted to him.

For children who wish a dog of their own, the parents have to cooperate and assist the child to make this possible. While the overall responsibility for the proper care, feeding and training must remain with the adult, the actual work process should be transferred to the child as much as age, size and ability permit. As a parent, I found this to be twice as much effort as just doing all the dog chores myself.

Nonetheless, the child should be the one who feeds the dog at regular hours, while the parent

Bullmastiffs enjoy playing with children, and the feeling is usually mutual.

checks to be sure the proper amount of food is given at the right time. Children should accompany the dog to the vet, learn to brush and bathe it and take part in the housetraining process. If dominance downs are practiced with the young puppy to teach control and bonding, the child should also do the exercise under the supervision

A puppy comfortably lounging in a suitable crate.

of a parent. The adult may train the dog, but again, a school-age child should also attend class with the dog, or at least practice at regular intervals.

All this requires perseverance and patience with both child and Bullmastiff. If the efforts succeed, there is a wonderful bond that lasts a lifetime. At the very least, you have a loving family companion.

THE DARK SIDE

Although the Bullmastiff is normally a great companion, there are negative aspects to the breed that should be understood. Some Bullmastiffs tend to be aggressive toward other dogs, and that characteristic unfortunately sometimes includes dogs that live in the same household.

Although there may sometimes be a problem between bitches or mixed sexes, the most common problems are between Bullmastiff males. Unless they are to be kennel dogs or are going to a very knowledgeable owner, most experienced breeders will not place two males in the same household. Although two males may appear to be best friends in most cases, the day finally arrives when the two dogs look at each other and, for some unknown reason, decide that the other must go. The situation immediately escalates to a fight, and from that point on the two should be religiously separated to prevent injury to each other or to the family members who might try to break up a fight or accidentally come between them. If there is no way to securely separate the antagonists, if there are young children in the home, if the owners cannot cope with a lifetime of rotating dogs and the very real danger of a fight, we recommend that one of the dogs be placed in a new home without other dogs, so that all involved, both canine and human, can enjoy a good quality of life.

If you own a more aggressive Bullmastiff, it is your responsibility to fully obedience train your dog, to anticipate and prevent fights from happening, and to never allow the dog to be in a situation where it can do harm.

There are some measures you can take in multi-dog homes. The most important is that the dog should always wear some sort of collar. Choke collars can be dangerous for day-to-day wear, but a flat

leather or woven nylon collar is safe and effective.
A dog without a collar is very difficult to safely grasp in an emergency.

If a fight breaks out, owners should place human safety first. It is also essential that children be taught they are not to attempt to break up a dogfight by themselves. They should also be told not to scream or shriek, which could make the fight worse, and they should be instructed to get an adult for help.

Sometimes a loud, angry shout from a dominant owner will cause the dogs to stop fighting, but in the heat of battle, it's not likely. A dowsing with cold water sometimes will have the desired effect. Pepper spray, designed for personal defense, has been reported very effective and leaves no serious side effects. We have kept it available in our multi-dog home for years, but have never had to use it. Although I am somewhat skeptical, a friend once told me that he stopped fights by covering the battling dogs with a large heavy blanket or a huge box.

My own worst fighter was a heavy, old-fashioned male Boxer who had a knack for escaping from the house or yard and raising havoc with the

While these young pups are fast friends, as they grow older it is unlikely they will be able to live together peacefully.

neighborhood dogs. To break up his encounters, we kept a four-foot wooden pole with a metal hook on the end that had originally been designed as an antique window latch. The pole could safely be inserted into the melee, hooked on the dog's collar, twisted to secure him and then the struggling dog could be extricated without danger of injury to anyone.

Since antique window latches are not easily available, a good substitute is a four-foot length of dowel or a broomstick handle with a sturdy hook or plant holder screwed into one end.

Please note, this approach only works when the aggressor is the one hooked and removed from combat. With Bullmastiffs, it might be wise to keep a pair of these hooks on hand.

Whatever method you use to stop a fight, it is essential that no one gets between two battling dogs. The dog might not recognize a human hand, arm or leg until it's too late. Very serious injury can result from this mistake, so don't make it! The best anti-dogfight advice is to be responsible, to train, to socialize and to be prepared.

(Henrik Eriksen)

CHAPTER 6

Routine Care

Bullmastiffs are an easier breed to care for than many. They are physically robust, and are good eaters. Basic good grooming for a Bullmastiff is simple and requires only a minimum of effort. There are no tails to dock, ears to crop, or coats to snip and shape, blow dry and fluff.

Of course that does not mean they don't need any care from their owners. Quite the contrary. You must pay attention to their diet, hygiene and health. We'll look at feeding and grooming in this chapter, and some health considerations in Chapter 7.

FEEDING AND SUPPLEMENTS

Feeding instructions should have been supplied when you acquired your puppy. Use the same food recommended by the breeder, and at first stick to the same basic feeding regimen the puppy was on in the kennel. Ordinarily, that means three to four meals of a high-quality dry dog food, with or without any additives recommended by the breeder.

If you have purchased a pup from an experienced breeder, let that experience be your guide in feeding your new arrival. If the breeder says to feed special puppy food or one of the new large-breed puppy foods, do it. If the breeder suggests immediately starting the pup on adult food, do so. And if they tell you to avoid certain brands of food because they have been unsuccessful with them in the past, pay attention. Benefit from a qualified breeder's expertise and experience when feeding your puppy, and take unsolicited advice from others with a proverbial grain of salt.

These pups are lean but not thin, with bright eyes and glossy coats.
Don't let your puppy grow too fat, or health problems could ensue.
(Helene Nietsch)

On the other hand, if the puppy came from an inexperienced or first-time breeder, it would be wise to seek out the opinions of experienced people who also own Bullmastiffs. Talk to your veterinarian, as well.

How much should you feed? Every dog is different, and you will have to watch your pup and make adjustments as needed. Begin by offering the eight- to 12-week-old puppy approximately one cup of food. If it eats that ravenously, the amount may be increased slightly. If it picks casually at its dinner and has not emptied its bowl in 20 minutes, remove the food and do not offer more until the next mealtime. A healthy puppy will not starve itself, but it might develop bad eating habits that will have you begging it to eat or catering to its whims for the rest of its life! Bullmastiffs are quite

perceptive about this sort of thing, so right from the beginning do not allow mealtime to become a battleground of wills.

After the pup has been in its new home a few days, you can logically make some adjustments, based on your observations. For instance, if the puppy eats a hearty breakfast and then wanes in enthusiasm as each subsequent meal arrives, it is being fed too often. Switch to one less meal per day and observe whether its appetite increases for the remaining meals.

Check periodically for proper weight and condition by grasping the pup's skin immediately behind the elbows (outer armpit) between your fingers and thumb. If it feels soft and padded, your puppy might be overweight. Although it is natural to feel pride in a rapidly growing puppy, fast growth and excessive weight are major contributors to unsoundness and developmental problems in Bullmastiffs. A lean puppy with bright eyes and a glossy coat growing at a smooth, even rate should be the ideal—not the cute, roly-poly, butterball.

In addition to food, it is absolutely essential that the pup drinks plenty of clean, fresh water. If it is not constantly accessible, water should be offered regularly during the day. Spill- and splash-proof water bowls with a firm-fitting cover with a hole in the center are available for the serious Bullmastiff dabbler, or "water rat."

Fewer and fewer modern Bullmastiff breeders are recommending vitamin and mineral supplements for their dogs. Premium-quality dog food has made supplementation with calcium and vitamins often unnecessary and sometimes detrimental if, for example, the ratio between calcium and phosphorus should become unbalanced. Unless strongly recommended by the breeder or prescribed by your veterinarian for some particular condition, generally avoid giving vitamins and calcium.

The one exception to this rule, particularly for fast-developing youngsters and pregnant and nursing bitches, seems to be the addition of vitamin C to the diet to promote healthy joint formation and provide other benefits. There is little scientific evidence to support the claims for vitamin C, but advocates swear by it. Those who supplement with it usually recommend non-acidic vitamin C in the form of sodium ascorbate, which must be purchased in a health food store or ordered by mail. The more readily available ascorbic acid seems to be slightly less effective.

Wash a Bullmastiff's face often, and make sure the skin in the folds of the wrinkles is kept dry. (Gail Painter)

cleanliness, brushing and nail trimming. Additionally, the ears should be cleaned, the teeth checked for tartar and the coat examined for parasites regularly.

A young puppy should have its face washed with a warm, wet cloth at least once or twice a day, or after each meal, with particular care being given to the area around the lips, chin and muzzle. This prevents food and bacteria from building up on the face or remaining in the wrinkles.

An adult dog should also have its face cleaned regularly, particularly if it tends to drool. A dirty face seems to pick up and hold more odor than the rest of the dog, so in addition to general cleanliness, face washing pays a dividend in making your pet more pleasant to be around—plus, the dog enjoys it.

Unless muddy or very dirty, the coat may also be kept clean with a weekly rubdown with a warm, wet towel, followed by a vigorous rub with a clean towel to dry.

House pets are fully bathed more frequently than dogs that spend most of their time outside. However, all dogs should be thoroughly bathed before a dog show, and before traveling or visiting away from home.

BRUSHING AND BATHING

Bullmastiffs are essentially considered wash and wear. The most important elements of care are

Phirene Dempsey is a well-groomed dog in the peak of physical condition. (Val Cole)

A small puppy fits nicely into the kitchen sink or laundry tub, but only for a few weeks. Washing an adult Bullmastiff is a bit more difficult. Few dog owners have separate canine bathing facilities, but the hand–held shower massage unit in the family bath can make washing much simpler. A basement laundry room with a floor drain and a garden hose hooked up to the sink also work well in colder weather. In the summer or on mild days, by far the easiest method is to bathe the dog outdoors. A hose can be attached to the kitchen or laundry faucet, adjusted for warm water, and the entire procedure may be accomplished without a major mess.

Farm and tack supply shops sell inexpensive plastic brushes that attach to the end of a garden hose. This tool sprays water into the coat and also massages and separates the hair to get the skin really clean and properly rinsed.

The job is easier if everything is prepared and on hand before you start the bath. Mix some of the chosen shampoo with a little warm water in a plastic cup. (Dog shampoo is really better for dogs than human shampoo, which can dry out the coat.) Completely wet the dog's coat. Starting at the back of the neck, work the diluted shampoo down, around and under toward the end of the tail, until the entire body has been lathered. Use a piece of terrycloth to wash the face, lips, chin, head and both sides of the ears. Some flea and conditioning shampoos are supposed to be left on the coat for a specific period of time, so be sure to read the directions on the bottle. Otherwise, rinse completely, starting at the head. If the coat was particularly dirty, there was a flea problem, or you used a special conditioning shampoo, you might wish to give a second shampooing to gain the full effect.

There should be absolutely no soap residue left in the hair after the rinse. If in doubt, rinse a second time. Towel off the excess water, allow the dog to shake, and then rub it down again with a thick, dry towel to finish the project.

The dog should be confined in a clean dry area, either indoors or out, until the coat is fully dry. Bullmastiffs are adept at finding the only dusty or muddy spot in the yard to roll in immediately after a bath. If the dog is confined to a crate after the bath, be sure to place a clean, fresh blanket down first. Unless you do so, the dog will pick up odors from the dampened bedding, even if it has only been in the crate a day or two.

When the coat is dry, groom with a soft brush and finish with a slicker tool.

If it is shedding season or the dog is losing its undercoat, use a metal shedding blade or a rubber curry comb to remove as much loose hair as possible *before* a bath. Afterwards, repeat the process. Bathing tends to loosen the shedding hair and will often hasten the process with a bit of judicious grooming.

Smooth-coated dogs like the Bullmastiff don't have the heavy shedding problems found in the longhaired breeds, but they do produce a fair

Bullmastiffs are adept at finding the dusty spots in the garden to dig and roll in, as soon as your back is turned. This is Oldwell Wayne with Ann Colliass.

Regular brushing will ensure a healthy coat and minimize the loose hair around the house. (Dominique DeVito)

amount of hair once or twice a year. This can be minimized by regular brushing and by using grooming tools to remove the loose hair when and where you prefer.

Using a flea comb before you brush will alert you to the presence of these parasites before they become a serious problem in the house or yard. Special attention should be given to the area around the neck and ears, along the back and especially at the base of the tail. Any fleas and debris removed on the comb should be rinsed off into a handy container of hot soapy water, and later flushed down the drain.

Brushing accomplishes two tasks: It keeps the coat and skin free of dirt and debris, and also serves as a pleasant pastime and another opportunity to touch and to bond with your dog.

CLIPPING NAILS

Nail trimming is probably the most neglected grooming operation. Starting when the puppy is small, you should trim its nails once a week. We use a large toenail clipper designed for humans on our newborns and tiny pups. As the nails grow and thicken, there are a variety of canine nail clippers available in pet supply stores and from catalogs.

Always cut just the hard part of the nail, avoiding the quick—the capillary inside the nail. If you accidentally nick the quick, you will see a little blood. Styptic powder, or, in a pinch, cornstarch, will quickly stop the bleeding. Remember that cutting a pup's nail won't hurt him, but cutting the quick will.

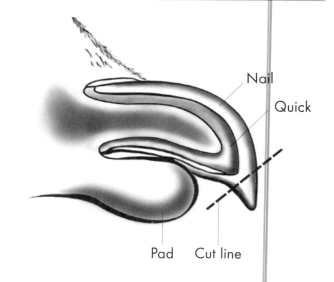

Simply cut on the dotted line.

Many Bullmastiffs instinctively struggle whenever their toenails are handled. Some seem far more sensitive to the cutting sensation than others, so it is important that they learn from a young age that this is a procedure to which they must submit, whether they like it or not.

Sometimes these super-sensitive dogs prefer to have their nails filed or ground with a lightweight hand-held electric or battery-operated power grinder. Grinders designed especially for dogs may be purchased from pet supply shops or catalogs, or small portable rotary tools with replaceable grinding heads, such as the Dremel, may be found in the hardware or tool section of many stores.

Using the high-speed grinder is quick and efficient, but care must be taken not to remove too much nail too quickly. Trim the nail as if you are paring an orange or apple, trying not to damage the underlying soft matter. Repeated, short touches to the nail from several angles gradually shape it, yet avoid discomfort to the dog from friction heat or nicking the quick.

Although not an ideal alternative, if a dog's nails have been neglected or allowed to grow too long, or if it refuses to allow you to attend to them, you may discuss the option of having it tranquilized and the nails cut back by a veterinarian.

(Gail Painter)

CHAPTER 7

Keeping Your Bullmastiff Healthy

Routine veterinary care is a must for every dog. That means your dog should visit the vet once a year, whether it is sick or not. It is the nature of dogs to hide any pain or illness they feel. This stoicism is inherited from the dog's wild ancestors, who could easily become prey if they showed any sign of weakness. Regular visits to the vet will help detect problems while they are still treatable.

Each new Bullmastiff puppy or dog should come with a health record showing which inoculations were given, the dates, and the name and lot number of the vaccine injected. The record should also include the same type of information on worming, medical tests, treatments, X-rays and procedures done before the sale.

You should also keep a written record of any pertinent medical information received from the breeder or previous owner about familial sensitivity or intolerance to any particular vaccine, drug or anesthetic. Make a copy of the health and inoculation records, along with any other notes concerning the dog's medical background, and give it to your dog's veterinarian. Keep the originals for your own files.

Unless the breeder has given you strong recommendations concerning inoculations, let the veterinarian be your guide in health matters for your dog. Vets often have differing opinions on preferred vaccines and the timing for shots, as well as the advisability of worming and giving preventives for such things as heartworm, Lyme disease in tick infested regions, and flea and tick control methods. A qualified veterinary practitioner is your best source of medical advice, just as the breeder often knows what is best concerning regular nutrition and husbandry.

INOCULATIONS

Common dog diseases, such as distemper, hepatitis, parvovirus, corona, leptospirosis and some strains of kennel cough can seriously debilitate or unnecessarily kill an uninoculated Bullmastiff. It makes no sense to put your dog at risk when a simple vaccine will ensure protection. Likewise, it is a foolhardy risk to omit recommended heartworm preventive and tick control medications for Lyme disease and Rocky Mountain spotted fever in areas where those problems are endemic.

Some countries do not have rabies at the present time, so they require no inoculations for the disease. However, in the United States and most other countries, rabies shots are required by law for all dogs. In areas where rabies outbreaks have been

Your dog depends on you, and it makes no sense to put it at risk for diseases that are easily prevented. (Gail Painter)

reported, proof of such inoculation may be required, and all owners traveling with their dogs should carry a copy of an up-to-date rabies certificate at all times. For the health of the dog, it is often suggested that rabies inoculations should be administered separately from other vaccines.

PUPPY EAR PROBLEMS

The cartilage in a Bullmastiff puppy's ears is very pliable. Sometimes during the rapid growth stage and teething, the ears will either "rose" (the ear folds over and back to reveal the inside) like a Bulldog's ear or "fly" (the ear stands up at the base but folds over at the tip) like a Whippet or Greyhound's ear. Neither is correct for the adult Bullmastiff, but often the ear will resume its proper carriage as the teething stage is passed. Other puppies must have their ears taped to encourage the ear cartilage to fold in the proper manner. It must not be allowed to stay folded incorrectly, as this greatly detracts from the overall appearance.

A roll of duct tape, rubbing alcohol and scissors are all that is needed to tape the ears. Inspect the puppy's ears to make sure they are clean and free of infection or mites. Then clean the inside and outside of the ear with alcohol. This is to remove the natural oil, which might prevent the tape from sticking to the ear. Duct tape (so named because it is used for taping the joints of air conditioning ducts) is normally found in three-inch widths. You will need to use half that width. Tear off or cut six strips that are one and one-half inches wide and are one inch longer than the puppy's ear (measured at the forward edge).

Place a strip on the inside forward edge of each ear, allowing the extra inch of tape to hang down.

Now place another strip of tape along the outside forward edge of each ear, also with an inch of tape extending off the tip of the ear. Press together the sticky sides of the one-inch strips.

Fold one ear properly, and attach another tape strip to the underside of the tab hanging from the tip of that ear (the sticky side will be facing out, not touching the dog's hair). Holding that ear folded properly, fold the other ear and run the tape strip under the dog's chin, attaching it to the underside of the tab on the other ear. The ears should now be pulled down and held just tightly enough that the cartilage fold is in the proper place. Attach the remaining strip of tape on the outside of the tape strip running under the chin, to reinforce the tape and to cover up the sticky side.

Leave the ears taped for about one to two weeks. Then gently remove the tape and clean the ears. Observe the ear carriage for 24 hours. If the

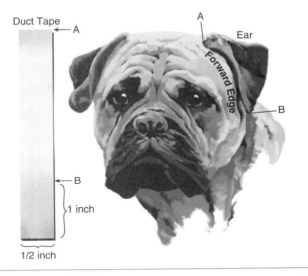

Measure the length of the ear from point A to point B, and then cut six strips of duct tape that are one inch longer.

Fasten tape strips to the underside of each ear.

Fasten tape strips on the top forward edge of each ear, and press together the extra tabs.

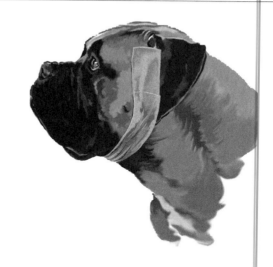

Be sure the creases on top of both ears are correct and the tape under the chin is tight enough to hold the ears flat.

ears remain folded properly, they will not need re-taping. If the ears return to their previous position, repeat the taping as necessary until the ears are carried properly.

WORMING

Most dogs contract worms or parasites of one sort or another at some point in their lives. Many puppies are born with roundworms or are infected with them soon after birth by nursing from the dam. Although parasite-free at the time of breeding or whelping, if she had been previously infected with roundworms, it is possible for encysted larva to be passed through the mammary tissues to the new puppies. Be sure to follow the recommendations of the breeder about how to

continue the worming program they initiated with your puppy.

Owners who routinely take their Bullmastiffs to shows, parks or other places frequented by dogs should consider a preventive plan to control these unhealthy parasites.

HEALTH CONCERNS

Bullmastiffs are a relatively healthy breed. However, there are some conditions that appear to be fairly commonplace in the breed. These include *allergies,* most commonly to fleas or a food ingredient; *entropian,* a sometimes painful condition where the eyelid turns slightly inward, causing the lashes to irritate the surface of the eye; *ectropian,* a condition where the lower eye lid sags outward; low thyroid function, known as *hypothyroidism; skin and coat problems,* including interdigital cysts; and *hip dysplasia,* which, although somewhat common in the Bullmastiff, may offer few symptoms or hints of its existence until discovered on an X-ray.

Hypothyroidism is a disease of the thyroid gland. It is usually considered to be genetic, although episodes of transient hypothyroidism may be caused by some medications or exposure to chemicals. The disease is usually manifested after a dog is two years old.

While it is normally treatable with medication, a conscientious breeder will attempt to eliminate or lessen its occurrence within their dogs. Because of the incidence of thyroid imbalance in Bullmastiffs, it is probably wise to request that tests be run sometime after puberty, at about one year for males and during anestrus (the time between heats) after a bitch's first season. Regular testing should then become a part of the dog's annual veterinary checkup and screening.

The condition is simple to treat and inexpensive to manage. Untreated hypothyroidism may cause alterations in cellular mechanisms, neuromuscular problems, dermatologic diseases, reproductive disorders, cardiac abnormalities, gastrointestinal disorders, hematological disorders, ocular diseases and various endocrinal disorders.

The outward symptoms a breeder notices first may be sluggishness, obesity, hair loss with skin darkening at the flanks or aggressive temperament.

Most authorities believe hypothyroidism is a polygenic disorder. This means the tendency toward the disease cannot be totally eliminated through simple Mendelian selection.

ORTHOPEDIC CONCERNS

It is not uncommon for a puppy or a growing adolescent to be afflicted with transient lameness from a condition known as *panosteitis.* This malady affects the long bones of the legs and may be revealed by X-ray. Pano is often misdiagnosed as a more serious orthopedic condition, such as hip dysplasia, either because of poor X-ray equipment or because the focus of the investigation is often the joints rather than the long bones of the legs.

Symptoms include pain or lameness that may come and go, or shift from leg to leg, and may be accompanied by low fever, listlessness or lack of appetite. The condition is self limiting, meaning the puppy will eventually fully recover. It has not been proven to be directly inherited. Treatment varies, but rest, anti-inflammatory medication such as aspirin, and occasionally antibiotics may be prescribed by the attending veterinarian.

Hip dysplasia can only be diagnosed by X-ray evaluation. Many Bullmastiffs that possess excellent movement, even when they are old, may have hip dysplasia, while a similar number might be certified as clear of the condition but still move like a spider on a hotplate.

Hip and elbow dysplasia are polygenic disorders of the hip and elbow joints. A dog may not manifest any outward sign of this disease in its early years, and its effects may or may not be visible as the dog ages. The only way to know for sure is by evaluation of X-rays.

There are two organizations in the United States that evaluate and certify X-rays sent to them by veterinarians. The oldest is the Orthopedic

The quick growth of younger dogs can cause transient problems with lameness. Regulating your pup's diet helps avoid this. (Dominique DeVito)

Foundation for Animals. This organization employs radiologists who evaluate the hips and elbows, and then issue a registry number to dogs that do not show with evidence of the disease. Dogs are rated Excellent, Good, Fair or Dysplastic, some supporting or explanatory information.

The newest evaluation technique in the war against hip dysplasia is PennHip, a different X-ray procedure named for the University of Pennsylvania Veterinary School where it was developed by Dr. Gale Smith and associates. PennHip has several advantages over the OFA program. It offers an objective measurement, instead of the more subjective evaluation given by OFA. PennHip does not rate the dogs, but furnishes a physical measurement of joint laxity from a series of X-rays. It then ranks the individual dog within a percentile, where it is compared to the overall population of its breed.

This joint laxity measurement can be an important breeder's tool, and, when coupled with the percentile ranking within the breed, gives breeders even more information on which to base decisions concerning breeding and showing. Generally, only males ranking in the top 50th percentile or higher should be used at stud. Breeding Bullmastiffs that are in the lower 50th percentile for the breed should be avoided.

There are other programs used in other countries. The British Veterinary Association has a scheme in which each individual hip is given a number. The idea of individually rating each hip has much merit. However, the BVA requirement that every evaluation be published and the inability to resubmit additional X-rays has resulted in many breeders refusing to have their stock X-rayed.

THE OLDER BULLMASTIFF

Hopefully, all beloved dogs will live to a ripe old age. Unfortunately, large dogs age faster than their smaller counterparts. The Bullmastiff, from about the age of seven years onward, may need somewhat different care than the younger dog.

It is sometimes a good idea to feed a kibble or a diet that is specially formulated for the older dog. This special dog food will normally have lower levels of protein and fat, while still supplying all the required nutrients. This will lighten the workload for the older dog's liver and kidneys and keep it from becoming too heavy for its aging joints.

You may also wish to give the older dog a softer bed and reduce the amount of exercise that the dog does not initiate itself. Walking and outdoor play are good for the oldster, but watch carefully for signs of fatigue if you are accustomed to jogging or engaging in strenuous activities together.

It is also necessary that the older dog's body be visually and manually checked periodically for skin problems and tumors. Be alert as you are petting and grooming your oldster, and look for any small lumps or bumps under the skin. Report these to your veterinarian immediately.

Nails may need more frequent attention because they tend to grow more quickly on an older dog due to the reduction in exercise. Footpads may become less tough, and in some cases seem to deflate or flatten with age. This causes the previously tight foot to splay a bit. Combined with longer nails, it can cause the formerly straight pasterns to bend or slope, creating more tension on tendons and joints. Older Bullmastiffs may lose up to an inch or more of their previous height.

Ch. Tauralan Queen Vic Toria is still trustworthy and on the job.

Check the teeth periodically for tooth and gum problems before they can become severe. If your dog suffers from arthritis or any other joint problems, the vet might recommend one of the newer daily supplements or medications to enhance his quality of life. These joint lubricators can bring a spring back to the step of an old timer. At this time they are fairly expensive for our large dogs, but are well worth the cost in many cases.

Old dogs often enjoy strong attachments with their families and with other pets in the household. They may sometimes grieve to the point of ill health at the death of an old companion or when the children go off to college. If such a major change occurs, give the dog more attention than usual to help ease him past the loss. You should also be watchful that a younger dog, in an attempt to move up the dominance ladder, does not exhibit aggressive behavior towards the older dog at such times.

Other than these few recommendations, simply continue the regular checkups by your veterinarian and enjoy your aging Bullmastiff. Count every day, month, and year as a special gift.

(American Kennel Club)

CHAPTER 8

Showing a Bullmastiff

Early dog shows were used as a way for breeders to compare and select the best dogs for their breeding stock. Although shows still perform the same function today, many Bullmastiff fanciers participate in showing as a competitive sport or as a fun hobby that can be shared with the family dog.

When compared with some of the more popular breeds, such as Poodles, a considerably high percentage of the Bullmastiffs bred in the United States are shown. Although campaigning a top dog to Group wins and Bests in Show can be very expensive and time consuming, attending a few shows or putting a championship on a deserving dog can be a fun and rewarding pastime.

Most of the shows in the United States, Canada and Great Britain are put on by individual clubs, and are held with the approval of the kennel club that governs registrations: the American Kennel Club (AKC), Canadian Kennel Club (CKC) and Kennel Club (KC). Each show also operates under the sanctioning organization's rules and regulations with regard to the breed standards, entries, classes, judging, grooming and the behavior of both dogs and exhibitors.

Dog shows range from tiny single-breed affairs with only a handful of entries to huge all-breed events, such as some of the Championship shows in Britain that attract more than 20,000 dogs. They may be held indoors or out, usually under tents or awnings. These shows often take on the appearance of large county fairs for dogs and fanciers. They are complete with many banners, concessions and vendors selling everything from leashes to art and jewelry. And all are vying for attention along with the more serious activities going on in the show rings.

FINDING A DOG SHOW

Dog shows in the United States and Canada are sponsored by a club, but are usually arranged by a professional dog show superintendent who is licensed by the AKC or CKC. Superintendents always try to publicize the shows they are arranging, so they can be a good source of information about what shows are coming up in your area. If you have access to the Internet, one way to find these superintendents is to search on the words "Dog Show Superintendent," and access their Web sites. The national kennel clubs also have Web sites, listed in Appendix F.

This multi-group placer, Ch. Flatiron's Julius Ceasar, owner-handled by Dana and Rick Wilhelm. He's an example of a first-time Bullmastiff owner being competitive in the show ring. (Wayne Cott)

upcoming shows. So does the *Events Calendar,* a supplement to the *AKC Gazette.* If you attend a show, you will have the opportunity to receive more information there directly from the superintendent or show secretary.

TRAINING FOR THE SHOW

If you bought a puppy with the idea of showing it, training should begin immediately. The best time of day for this is about halfway between feeding times. This early training program starts with teaching the puppy to be alert and look at you on command. To accomplish this, when the puppy is relaxed

Another way to find out when there will be shows in your area is to telephone the kennel clubs' information number (you'll find them in Appendix F, too) and ask about show superintendents and upcoming shows. It is also wise to request their booklet on dog shows and showing, and to ask for the name and phone number of the closest all-breed dog club.

Dog World, which is sold on many newsstands, has a list of superintendents and lists a number of

make a noise in your throat and say, "look at me" or "watch me." When the puppy responds, reward its attention with a treat. Practice this several times a day until it becomes alert whenever the sound is made or it hears the command.

Before starting to seriously train your puppy or dog for the show ring, you'll need the proper equipment. Measure the circumference of your dog's neck, as well as the circumference of the head at a point just in front of the ears. Purchase a nylon

Dogs compete in the Bred by Exhibitor Class at the American Bullmastiff Association national specialty. Specialty shows feature just one breed.

These can be commercially prepared dog snacks or bits of cooked liver, meat or cheese. A simple and inexpensive tidbit for puppies is chips of thinly sliced hot dogs that have been cooked in a microwave oven until dry and crisp. The main point is that whatever is used should be something the dog regards as a special treat.

Patience must be the watchword when training dogs for the show ring. Positive reinforcement when the dog does something right is vital for a show dog—or any dog. This positive reinforcement may come in the form of praise or the more tangible reward of food. Do not scold or punish the dog in these early stages of show training.

The best way to begin training is to put the dog in its crate for about an hour. When the hour is up, release it from the crate, put the show equipment on, and take it to an area where there are few distractions, especially from other dogs.

To teach your Bullmastiff to stand in a show pose, called stacking, stand it on your left side. Gather up the lead with your left hand and grip the collar with your right hand. Then move the gathered lead into your right hand as well, and reach over and down the front on the left side of the dog. Take the left front leg by the elbow and place the foreleg so that the foot, elbow and withers are in a straight line and perpendicular to the floor. Transfer the gathered lead and collar from the right hand to the left. Then grasp the elbow of the

or chain slip-ring collar that is two inches longer than the greater of those two measurements.

The best collars for the show ring are the metal, flat link, choke collars with the links measuring approximately one quarter of an inch long. The two inches of extra length give enough slack to control and correct the dog, while preventing the collar from sliding down around the shoulders.

The second piece of equipment you'll need is a sturdy nylon lead with a button slide snap. Remember that although your dog may not be aggressive, the lead must be strong enough to withstand a sudden jerk if the dog should be startled or needs to avoid another dog.

The third and final items needed for training are some small, easily eaten treats for the dog.

right foreleg with the right hand and place it so that the leg is in the same alignment from the withers to the foot. Once again, transfer the gathered lead to the right hand.

After the dog has stood in this position for a few seconds, say "OK," pat it on the chest and give it a tidbit. Then walk it around in a circle and repeat the stacking.

Work towards having the dog hold the pose for longer and longer as it begins to understand what is wanted. If it breaks the pose before being released, do not offer a tidbit. Make a soft noise in your throat to indicate the mistake, and then smoothly re-stack the dog, being sure to release it before it can make another mistake.

Repeat the cycle of stacking and rewarding at intervals during the next few days until your dog will reliably remain in position until released. This cannot be accomplished at one or two training sessions. Do not make the common error of pushing the dog too fast and hard. Bullmastiffs get bored easily, so keep the training time short, and always end with a successful performance and its resulting treat. Make the training

Ch. Laird of Oldwell is nicely stacked to show him off to his best advantage. (CS Photography)

sessions enjoyable, and you will find your dog will like to show.

When the dog has reached the point where it will reliably stand in position after having its front stacked, it is time to train it to have its rear stacked. Stack its front end as usual. Then, taking the gathered lead and collar in your right hand, reach over or under the dog (depending upon your height) and hold the dog by the point of the left hock (the first joint above the knee). Lift slightly and set the foot so that the hock is perpendicular to the ground.

While still holding the lead and collar in your right hand, set the right rear leg in the same manner.

Repeat your practice as with the front, gradually increasing the time the dog is required to remain in the stack. Do not forget to reward all successful tries, and again, do not push the dog too fast. It may be helpful to start using the word "stay" after placing the fourth leg in place.

When you are confident the dog will stay once it has been stacked, release the collar and, taking the end of the lead, move slightly away. As practice becomes steadier, you may step out in front of the dog while requiring it to remain in its pose. Take a piece of what-ever you have been using for a reward, step in front of the dog and roll the treat around in your fingers. If it has been taught "watch me," the command will teach the concept quickly. The object is to get the dog's attention and for it to become alert without leaving the stacked show position. This is called free-baiting, and will probably require many repeti-tions and rewards before it is mastered.

It is most important not to lose patience with the dog at this point. You will find that it seems as if you are mak-ing great progress when suddenly your dog will act as if it were the first lesson all over again. This is normal for the Bullmastiff, and this "on again, off again" behavior will likely repeat itself over and over during training, and even later in the show ring. Patience and a good sense of humor will help at such times.

Practice making adjustments at home so you can easily adjust your dog's position in the ring to make sure it looks its best. (American Kennel Club)

When you feel you and the dog have become proficient at stacking and free-baiting, try to enlist the help of a friend with a video camera. Video-tape the whole sequence of you setting up the dog in the stack and free-baiting it. Make sure you get views from both the side and the rear. Review the videotape and decide what adjustments should be made to improve the overall picture of you and your dog.

After mastering the art of free-baiting, it is time to work on the next step: gaiting the dog. Four basic gaiting patterns are most commonly used at dog shows. In the down and back, dog and handler move straight away to the end of the ring, turn around and return straight back toward the judge, stopping about three feet away from the judge. In the triangle, the dog is moved straight away from the judge to the end of the ring, then you make a left turn and go straight to the corner of the ring, followed by another left turn, and straight back along the diagonal of the triangle towards the judge, again stopping three feet from the judge. In the L-shaped pattern, the dog is gaited straight away from the judge to the end of the ring, then you make a left turn and gait to the corner of the ring. But instead of returning along

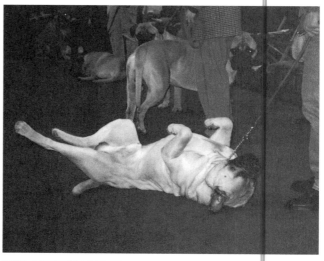

The most important thing to remember at a dog show is that you love your dog no matter what. (American Kennel Club)

A good sense of humor is a great asset in the show ring. This is Ch. Dajean Goldust the Poachersfoe.

the diagonal, the steps are retraced back along the path of the L until you've stopped in front of the judge. The fourth pattern is a circle around the perimeter of the ring. In all cases, when you return to the judge, get the dog's attention and make sure it is alert and focused.

Always try get to the ring in time to observe the patterns the judge is asking from the handlers and dogs in earlier classes. Most judges are consistent from breed to breed, and certainly from class to class, so by observing their gaiting patterns and ring procedures in advance, you will have more time to concentrate on making your dog look and move at its best.

The dog is always gaited on your left side with the lead held in your left hand. It is permissible to hold it in your right hand across the front of your

body. When gaiting the dog, do not let it surge ahead or drag back. The ideal is for its head to be only slightly ahead of your legs. Do not allow it to pull on the lead; this will make its rear appear faulty.

It is considered very bad manners to run up on the dog that is in front of you. If the dog in front is moving slower than the speed your dog looks best at, hold back and let a space open between you, then move your dog at the speed you think best. If the handler behind you is allowing his or her dog to run up on you, stop and indicate that the handler should go in front of your dog. Should the judge ask why you stopped, politely inform the judge that your dog was being interfered with by the animal behind. Keep in mind that Bullmastiffs were not built to be efficient at the trot, and they seldom look their best trotting at a high speed.

GROOMING FOR THE SHOW RING

Very little extra grooming is required to get your Bullmastiff ready to show. However, one area that cannot be skimmed over is cleanliness. Bullmastiffs with oily coats, and those kenneled outside, are usually the most offensive.

The dog should be thoroughly bathed immediately before each show or show weekend, using a good conditioning and deodorizing pet product or a dandruff shampoo. Be sure all traces of the shampoo are thoroughly rinsed from the coat. When the dog's coat has dried completely, check to see if any doggy odor remains. If the dog does smell, repeat the bath, this time using a coat conditioner in the rinse. A dog's chances in the show ring may be greatly hampered if the judge is reluctant to touch the dog due to a foul, unpleasant odor from its coat.

The nails should have already been trimmed, but may be shaped or filed lightly before a show. Nail trimming should be an ongoing process, so unless they are quite long, do not do any major trimming immediately before a show. If you do and accidentally cut into the quick, the dog may limp or pick up an infection in the nail at the show.

There are two schools of thought regarding the trimming of whiskers. Some handlers (mainly the professionals) cut the whiskers, but there is a growing number of handlers who leave the

This is Ch. Big Sur of Bull Brook, a great dog in top condition. (Alfred Stillman)

whiskers on the dog. Except in the stiffest of competition or when competing in the Group or Best in Show ring, whiskers should not affect the placement of the dog one way or another.

Never use any artificial color enhancers on the coat, mask, ears, nose or nails. Any product or procedure that changes the dog's natural appearance, including the use of artificial colorants, is universally forbidden and, if discovered, will disqualify the dog. Its handler and owner may also face suspension and a fine by the sanctioning organization.

Likewise, surgical procedures to correct entropian, osteochondritis dissecans (OCD, a joint disease), dental malocclusions, or to change the carriage of the tail or the size and set of the ears, render a dog ineligible to be shown. Each country has exempted certain kinds of surgery and procedures for the health of the dog. These are permitted even for show dogs.

THE CLASSES AT A DOG SHOW

Dog shows in the United States are arranged so that the dog that wins Best in Show has come through a series of classes in breed judging and won its Group. The chart on page 91 shows the path the top dog in a show must take to be named Best.

In addition, American and Canadian Kennel Club shows may offer a Veterans Class for dogs that are above a specified age, and Brood Bitch and Stud Dog classes, where the dogs are judged on the quality and consistency of their offspring.

The Winners Dog, Winners Bitch, winner of the Veteran Classes for dogs and bitches, plus all the finished Champions (called "specials") compete for Best of Breed.

In the United States, a neutered dog or a spayed bitch may not compete in conformation classes, except for the Stud Dog and Brood Bitch Classes or in the Veteran Classes at an independently held specialty show. The wise owner and exhibitor will be fully familiar with all the

Ch. Sunnybrook Sweet Sarah, a great bitch in top condition. (Tatham Photo)

governing rules pertaining to showing and registration in their country.

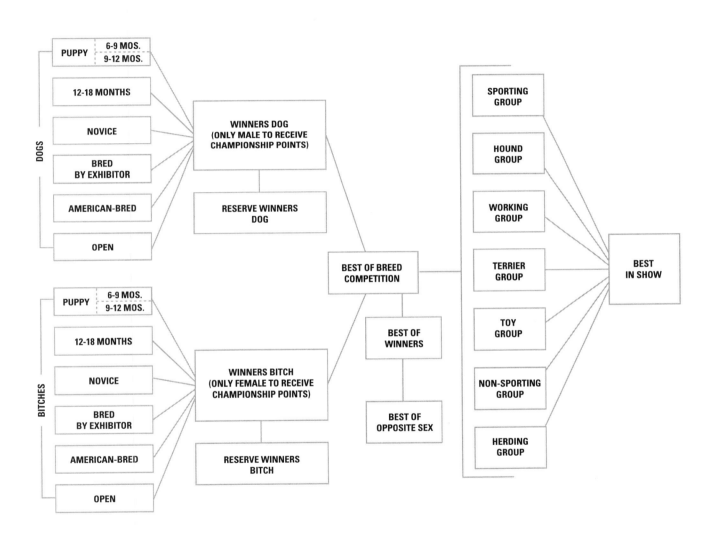

(Shirley LaFlamme)

CHAPTER 9

What Can You Do with a Bullmastiff?

The answer is, plenty. Bullmastiffs are active, intelligent dogs, and they love to have something to do. The AKC sports of Obedience, Tracking and Agility are open to Bullmastiffs. Other activities, including pet-assisted therapy, are as rewarding for you as they are for the dog.

In all of these activities, dogs with Limited Registration and those that are spayed or neutered are definitely welcome.

THE BULLMASTIFF AS A CANINE GOOD CITIZEN

Many countries now offer a version of the Canine Good Citizen (CGC) program, developed to encourage people to train their dogs. In the United States the program is administered by dog clubs and community-minded organizations, under the auspices of the AKC. The program is based on 10 tests, each designed to show that dogs can be well behaved at home, in public and around other dogs.

The tests measure the dog's ability to walk calmly on a leash, be approached by strangers and other dogs, wait quietly and come when called. Most Bullmastiffs living as companions and pets should be able

Every dog should be under control at home, outside and around other dogs. The Canine Good Citizen program is a great way to attain that goal.

to perform the very simple elements required to earn their CGC without any training beyond the basics every dog should have.

The title CGC does not appear on a dog's AKC pedigree, as regular Obedience titles do, but it is a starting point and is very rewarding for dog and owner.

THE OBEDIENCE BULLMASTIFF

An Obedience dog is not just a Bullmastiff that obeys its owner's commands. It is a dog that has been trained and has competed at some level for an Obedience title.

Obedience trials test a dog's ability to perform a set of exercises that are scored by a judge. Competition in the Obedience ring is divided into three levels, each more difficult than the previous one. At each level a competitor is working for an AKC Obedience title. The three levels and titles are:

- Novice: Companion Dog (CD)
- Open: Companion Dog Excellent (CDX)
- Utility: Utility Dog (UD)

Work at the Novice level includes the basic training that all dogs should receive to be good companions. Dogs need to demonstrate heeling both on- and off-leash at different speeds, coming when called, staying with a group of other dogs when instructed to do so and standing for a simple physical examination.

Open, the second level, is similar to Novice but requires the dog to perform off-leash and for longer periods. There are also jumping and retrieving tasks. The final level, Utility, adds still more difficult exercises, and the dog must also perform scent discrimination tasks.

The best of the best may go on to earn more titles. A Utility Dog that earns qualifying scores in both the Open B and Utility B Classes at 10 different events becomes a Utility Dog Excellent (UDX). Utility Dogs that are ranked first or second in Open B or Utility classes can earn points toward an Obedience Trial Champion (OTCh) title. (B classes are for experienced handlers, while A classes are for beginners whose dogs have never received a title.)

The Obedience rings have long been dominated by Golden Retrievers, Border Collies and Poodles, for good reason. Frankly, the desired level of independence inherent in the Bullmastiff usually

As long as the work is kept interesting, many dogs enjoy competing in Obedience. This is Ch. Elysian Albert Einstein Jr., CDX, with Mona Lindau-Webb.

precludes it from the stellar performances seen in more submissive and less easily bored breeds.

Generally, the Bullmastiff excels at the long sits and downs, is steady for the stand for examination, but tends to unravel a bit on the heeling exercises. At the more advanced levels, some difficulty may be encountered with retrieving the dumbbell. Although heeling is apt to be better when a dog reaches the Open class, it still remains the area where the most points are lost.

Still, if not bored to death by constant repetition, and if handled and trained correctly, the Bullmastiff can be a steady and interesting performer in the Obedience ring. Quite a few have earned their Utility titles (see Appendix D for a list).

For the Bullmastiff fancier who likes to be first at something that is a serious challenge, please note that there has never been an Obedience Trial Champion, or OTCh Bullmastiff in the United States, nor has one acquired the newest AKC title of UDX—yet. There have been several Bullmastiffs to earn a Canadian OTCh, but the requirements are not the same as for the AKC title.

At a time when Obedience entries are generally dropping for all breeds across the country, it is comforting to see that the Bullmastiff is becoming a more and more common sight at all levels in the Obedience ring. Several Bullmastiffs have succeeded in garnering legs toward their UD titles during the past year.

Conformation and Obedience are also coming to terms, with many dogs gaining a title at both ends of their name. Ch. Shastid's Beefeater Phred, CD, and Ch. Jubilee Captain Fantastic, CD, are credited with being the first Group-placing Bullmastiffs with Obedience titles.

As we write, a proposal is being considered by the American Kennel Club to include Bullmastiffs in a group of breeds that are required to jump heights that are within two inches of three-quarters of their height at the withers in the advanced levels of Obedience. Bullmastiffs are not great jumpers, and this change may encourage others to attempt

OBEDIENCE HISTORY MAKERS

The first Bullmastiff Companion Dog title was earned in 1947 by Pocantico Snowshoe, CD (Pocantico Pathfinder out of Princess Chloe), owned by Edith Pyle. In the next ten years only four more Bullmastiffs attained the title.

In 1958 a bitch named Boadicea (William of Oreland out of Diana of Harford), owned by Mr. and Mrs. Walter Pidgeon, won the first Companion Dog Excellent.

Few Bullmastiff owners have been sufficiently interested in Obedience competition to take their dogs all the way to the Utility level. In 1960 Ch. Dark Gem of Sunnyhill, UD, ROM (Hambledon Red Boy out of Ch. Sabina Hadriana), owned by Joan and Earl Davis, became the first American Bullmastiff to earn a UD. Gem completed both her CDX and her UD titles in five trials. She had the further distinction of being the first dual title holder (conformation and Obedience), and later earned a Register of Merit award as the dam of seven champions. She died at nearly 13 years of age in 1970. Her sister, Naughty Jill of Sunnyhill, CDX, also did quite well in the Obedience ring.

Dark Gem's impressive record of Obedience, conformation and whelping box success was not to be duplicated for more than 20 years, by Ch. Watch Hill's Evita, UD, ROM (Watch Hill's Bristol Cream out of Ch. Arborcrest Quick Silver), owned by Joel and Mary Ann Duchin. Better known as Margo, she was the Duchin's second Utility Bullmastiff—their first was Lady Travis of the Bluegrass, UD.

The first Bullmastiff UD in Canada was Ch. Silver's Golden Treasure, OTCh, who earned her title in 1975. She was trained and shown by Tom McClintock.

to progress beyond the elementary level of Obedience showing.

TRACKING WITH BULLMASTIFFS

Tracking trials allow dogs to demonstrate their natural ability to recognize and follow human scent. During a trial, a person gets up very early in the morning and lays down a track by walking a specified course, dropping a personal item, such as a glove, at the end. Later in the day, the dog must find and follow the track.

As in Obedience, there are three levels of competition. A dog earns a Tracking Dog (TD) title by following a complex track laid by a person 30 minutes to two hours before the event. To earn a Tracking Dog Excellent (TDX) title, a dog must successfully follow a track that is older, longer and less direct, while overcoming physical and scenting obstacles. Finally, a dog that can track through urban settings as well as through wilderness can earn a Variable Surface Tracking (VST) title. A VST dog demonstrates this ability by following a three- to five-hour-old track over a variety of surfaces, such as down a street, through a building and across a lot.

The first Bullmastiff to earn an AKC tracking title was Ch. Lady V's Hot Shot Shelah, CDX, TD,

Ch. Oakridge Luke Skywalker, UD, clearly enjoys his flight over the bars at an Obedience trial.

in 1978. She was owned by Peggy Graham and bred by Denise L. Borton, and attained TDs in both the United States and Canada. Peggy wrote in the August 1983 *ABA Bulletin,* "There is no more solitary and time-consuming training than that of tracking. Arising before dawn and venturing into the elements in all kinds of weather, these dogs and handlers deserve special recognition. This aspect of Obedience is unique in that the handler has no idea if the dog is performing his task." Such work requires a special bond of trust between handler and dog.

THE AGILITY BULLMASTIFF

Agility competition is a new sport for the AKC Bullmastiff. Agility trials allow a dog to demonstrate its ability to negotiate a complex course that includes walking over a bridge, weaving in and out of a series of poles, jumping through and over objects, traversing tunnels and pausing on command. There are different height categories for the jumps, so each dog can be tested fairly.

There are three classes at an agility trial: Novice, Open and Agility Excellent. The course is the same for every class, but the scoring gets more and more demanding as you progress through the classes.

To acquire an agility title, a dog must earn a qualifying score in its class at three different trials

THE TRACKING CHAMPS

Bullmastiff tracking dogs, as a group, are extraordinary in that they are all dual title holders. Ch. Echoing Oaks Cherubim, (Can) TD, owned by Craig Pelletier, earned her Canadian title in the same year as Shelah. The second AKC tracking title was earned five years later by Ch. Diamond Jim Brodie, CD, TD. He was owned by Terry and Marti Gould. There have been only five additional Bullmastiffs to achieve their tracking titles since that time: Am./Can. Ch. Boldwinds Taurus, TD; Ch. Pretty Boy Harry, TD; Ch. Shady Oaks Cassie, CD, TD; Ch. Shady Oaks Days of Glory CD, TD; and the multi–Best in Show bitch, Ch. Ladybug's Lady Caitlin, TD.

The pause table is one of the agility exercises. Ch. Ol' West Golden Rose of Cheyenne practices here with Gayle.

Caitlin at work on a track.

under two different judges. The titles earned at AKC agility trials are Novice Agility (NA), Open Agility (OA), Agility Excellent (AX) and Master Agility Excellent (MX).

Agility for Bullmastiffs is practically unknown in Britain, where the sport is dominated by flashing-fast Border Collies and the like. However, American fanciers have embraced the sport in surprising numbers. Many have found it to be a wonderful outlet for their dogs' energy and spirit. Perhaps the reason Bullmastiffs take to the sport so enthusiastically is that the activity resembles the type of early training given to the fledgling Night Dogs by the gamekeepers so long ago.

The American Bullmastiff Association National Specialty show included an Agility trial for the first time in 1997. Thirteen dogs participated.

Most dogs love to run agility courses, and Keeper's Anne Bonney, CD, MX, is no exception. (Cindy Noland)

AGILITY HEADLINERS

Mona Lindau Webb's bitch, Tauralan Tequila Sunrise, better known as Tiki Wiki, was the first to earn the NA title. Shortly afterwards, Ch. Ironwood's Buffalo Bill Cody, CD, owned by Mark and Barbara Brooks Worrell, became the first male NA. Keeper's Anne Bonney, CD, MX, became the first of the breed to attain Agility's highest title in 1997. She is owned and handled by Shirley La Flamme, and was bred by Anne and Cledith Lewis.

BULLMASTIFFS AT YOUR SERVICE

Bullmastiffs excel as therapy dogs. Their calm demeanor and ability to respond to different people and situations make them an ideal large breed for therapy work. In 1987, the Bullmastiff Jake and his partner, Micky Niego, were honored at the Gaines Assistance Animals Awards as the Delta Society Therapy Dog of the Year. The awards honored outstanding achievements of service and therapy animals that assisted physically and mentally disabled people. Jake served as the model dog for the American Society for the Prevention of Cruelty to Animals' program for pet-assisted therapy. He also assisted handicapped children and adults during countless visits to hospitals, schools and nursing homes. More than 10 years later, Micky is still working in pet therapy with the young Bullmastiffs that follow in Jake's pawprints.

Since that time many other Bullmastiffs and their owners have devoted countless hours to therapy visits. Therapy has also become an increasingly popular activity for retired Bullmastiff show-ring Champions, allowing them to continue to enjoy the limelight with a whole new type of audience. Several years ago during the televising of the Westminster Kennel Club Show, one such dog was profiled. Ch. Mr. U's Music Man, the multi–AKC Best in Show winner and former Number One Bullmastiff of the Year, was shown in his new role

Ch. Ol' West Lily Langtree and Kris practice the A-frame. Agility exercises are not unlike the early training gamekeepers gave their Night Dogs.

Micky Niego and Ch. Igor's Thunder Road Gowanis, CD, TT, CGC, accept their award from the Delta Society.

as therapy dog, visiting hospitals with his daughter, Ch. Mr. U's Hello Dolly.

Training for therapy visits is not rigorous, and allows most friendly, well-behaved Bullmastiffs to quickly become productive therapy dogs in a modest amount of time.

Bullmastiffs have also been trained to serve in various capacities as assistance dogs to their disabled owners. Although rarely used as guide dogs for the blind because of their size and bulk, a growing number have been trained to assist their hearing-impaired owners, as well as those suffering from diseases such as diabetes and epilepsy. And a Bullmastiff with a responsive nature and a natural instinct to retrieve objects can be of great help to owners who are confined to wheelchairs.

Bullmastiffs employed in these occupations require specialized training, and sometimes must also earn some type of official certification before the dog may be considered a service dog that is permitted full access to all stores, restaurants and public buildings.

BULLMASTIFFS TO THE RESCUE

There are several Bullmastiff search-and-rescue teams currently working in North America and Europe. The breed's naturally good nose and its affinity for tracking make the Bullmastiff a good candidate for this type of work. This is the ultimate challenge of the dog's training, conformation and endurance. Search-and-rescue (SAR) dogs may help in the hunt for a lost hiker or a wandering child, seek the location of a drowning victim or search for survivors in demolished buildings following a major disaster such as an earthquake or explosion.

Search and rescue demands a great commitment in time and training from the handler, and stretches the endurance and abilities of the Bullmastiff to the maximum. Carrie Dornan from British Columbia, Canada, reports that training involves up to 15 to 20 hours of training and conditioning a week for both dog and handler, and it may take from three to four years to completely train a reliable SAR dog.

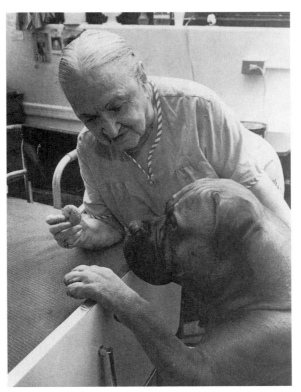

Jake waits patiently until Rose tells him it's OK to have the cookie.

Her dog, Honch, was started with training for a TD tracking title, and then proceeded to the more specific search-and-rescue training for urban and wilderness tracking; air-scenting scenarios; lost article recovery; road, water and dead-end crossings; major contaminant factors; and cadaver recovery.

With the relatively short life span of the Bullmastiff, the potential search-and-rescue dog is best selected and trained from puppyhood. A search-and-rescue prospect should be outgoing, responsive, easily motivated and keen. Some basic puppy tests and problem-solving exercises help to identify pups with the necessary prerequisites of intelligence, temperament and scenting ability.

Sound conformation, moderate size within the standard, good feet and excellent natural movement are essential to a dog that will be asked to work over rough terrain in all kinds of conditions. Adequate angulation front and rear will help to avoid later disappointments and injuries. The potential SAR Bullmastiff should also come from a pedigree with sound hips and elbows, and be free of other health concerns.

(Amy Hayward)

CHAPTER 10

Responsible Breeding

Just as not all Bullmastiffs should be exhibited at dog shows, not all Bullmastiffs should be bred—not even all good ones! In this age of unwanted dogs and crowded animal shelters, a true dog lover will carefully examine the reasons for contemplating a litter and only proceed for some very, very good reasons.

Wanting to make back what you paid for your dog is not one of them. Be assured that breeding dogs is an expensive hobby. Any idea of making a profit should immediately be discarded, because when breeding is done properly, the expense usually greatly exceeds the income.

You have a much greater chance of success if your emphasis is on breeding good-quality dogs that conform to the Bullmastiff standard, rather than on any anticipated monetary gains. Forget about breeding your family pet to the convenient dog down the street to get back what you paid for it or to earn a little extra spending money. Although it may sound harsh, if a person who deliberately breeds dogs is not sincerely concerned about responsibility and the good of the breed, then they are part of the problem for Bullmastiffs, rather than part of the solution.

Do you feel a commitment to protect the quality of the breed and to contribute to its welfare? Is your Bullmastiff a quality animal that conforms closely to the standard of excellence? Is it sound in temperament and body, with no known major or chronic health problems? Have all the normal screening procedures been completed to ensure that it is free of genetic diseases, hip and elbow dysplasia, hereditary eye defects and hypothyroidism? Do *you* have sufficient knowledge and background in the breed, or at least an experienced Bullmastiff mentor to help advise and assist you in planning the breeding? Are you prepared for the real labor and expense of rearing a litter, perhaps keeping all of the pups for many months until just the right homes are available? Are you willing to be responsible for the puppies that you produce, for the rest of their lives? Only consider breeding if you can answer yes to every single one of these questions.

THE BITCH

If you are determined to become a Bullmastiff breeder, it is prudent to start with the best stock available. This usually means buying a show- and breeding-quality female. If your first Bullmastiff is simply a pet or has major faults, it is best to accept the fact that she is not of sufficient quality to improve the breed and do not try to "make do" by breeding her. Instead, buy another bitch that is of excellent show and breeding stock for the foundation of your line. This will allow you to start level with the rest of the successful and ethical breeders.

To select a potential show- and breeding-quality bitch, you must first become fully acquainted with the Bullmastiff standard. If you have already purchased a show- and breeding-quality bitch, the next step is to assess what you have to work with. Anyone planning to become a breeder should get a copy of the AKC videotape *The Dog in Motion*. This is one of the best sources of information available to a breeder about proper canine structure and movement. The video reviews elements of structure and illustrates how good and bad conformation affects the corresponding movement. The

The scrutiny of the show ring will help you decide if you have a bitch of breeding quality. This is Ch. Todomas Naomi. (Dave Freeman)

Bullmastiff is a working dog and should move efficiently. Understanding structure and movement

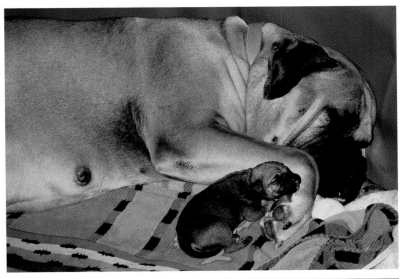

There's nothing like a puppy face!

Bullmastiffs usually make good mothers.

A Bullmastiff is a large, exuberant dog, and needs plenty of exercise and activity. (Gail Painter)

Bullmastiffs look great wherever they go. Gordon del Bullrotcan lives in Spain.

Chew toys are a must for any puppy. Ch. Ladybug Essex at Shastid loves his stuffed animals.

will assist a breeder in evaluating the areas in which their bitch might need to be compensated in the choice of a stud dog.

We also highly recommend that you exhibit your bitch and try to get her Championship *before* you breed. Introduce yourself to the other Bullmastiff fanciers at the show. At the very least, this activity will allow you to compare the quality of your bitch with that of the other show and breeding animals, to be sure she is really as good as you think and hope she is. Also, going to shows will give you a chance to observe and evaluate potential stud dogs.

Before you even consider breeding your bitch, you should have her hips evaluated. There is no way to effectively evaluate hips or elbows without an X-ray. Have your veterinarian also examine her eyes and draw a blood sample for thyroid and brucellosis tests well before she is due to come into season. All inoculations should be up to date, and the potential mother should be free of internal and external parasites. The bitch must not be fat, or it is possible that conception will be difficult if not impossible. Any excess weight should be shed well before breeding time.

Research has revealed that supplementation with folic acid reduces neural tube defects and other birth defects in humans. Studies have not been done with dogs. However, anecdotal evidence suggests folic acid may be helpful in preventing birth defects such as cleft palates and spinal deformities. Some breeders also supplement their bitches with vitamin C before and during pregnancy and lactation.

BREEDING STRATEGIES

One good way to start an animated discussion among dog fanciers is to compare the relative merits and pitfalls of inbreeding, line breeding and out-crossing. *Inbreeding* is the close breeding of related dogs, such as parent with offspring or brother with sister. Some breeders also consider a half-brother and half-sister match as inbreeding. Inbreeding Bullmastiffs requires great knowledge, skill and experience, and should not be attempted by novices. It is done to set certain characteristics found in the parents and other relatives. Since it brings out both the good and the bad, inbreeding may also be used as a test to discover some genetic strengths or flaws. To inbreed dogs, a person needs a good basic knowledge of canine genetics and an in-depth knowledge of related dogs and their pedigrees.

Line breeding, sometimes called strain breeding, is the breeding of less closely related Bullmastiffs. These may include breedings back to a grandparent, cousin to cousin, or uncle or aunt to nephew or niece. The term may also be used for looser line breedings where there are common ancestors found within a three- to five-generation pedigree. This method of breeding is frequently practiced by people who have a recognizable line of dogs and wish to make ongoing, subtle changes to improve the conformation or quality of the dogs produced. There is a better chance of success using this method when the dogs share some consistency of type.

Out-crossing is breeding dogs that have no common ancestors in a four- or five-generation pedigree. It is the less predictable method of breeding. Although safe, it usually produces less consistency in the offspring and in succeeding generations.

Best-to-best breeding may include any of the above strategies. It is breeding the best bitch to the best Bullmastiff male you can find, regardless of their pedigrees.

It should be noted that just about all Bullmastiffs in the world today are descended from the same animals. This would become readily apparent if the pedigrees were to be fully extended. Great dogs of the past, such as Farcroft Fidelity, Ch. Branch of Bulmas, Ch. Rodenhurst Masterpiece, Ch. Hickathrift Ra of LeTasyll and Ch. Ambassador of Buttonoak, will be found in nearly all Bullmastiff pedigrees.

SELECTING THE STUD DOG

The foremost principle in planning a breeding is that under no circumstances should you breed your bitch to a dog of lesser quality. If this simple tenet is not followed, the quality of your breeding program will deteriorate, or at the very least, will be at a standstill. And if your program is not improving the breed, there is no point in breeding.

The stud dog must be a good representative of the breed. Compare pedigrees to learn if and how the two dogs might be related. If they are, be sure the common ancestors are dogs you would like to reproduce.

Look for a male that complements your bitch. Together the pair should share many of the same outstanding characteristics and strengths. Breed for positive qualities rather than just to eliminate faults. However, ideally each will be able to compensate for any weaker point in the other. Avoid breeding to extremes. If the bitch is small, do not breed to a dog that is over the standard, expecting to gain height for the puppies. More likely the result will be some too small and some too tall, with very few in the correct range. Likewise, don't breed to an overshot dog to correct an undershot mouth, or breed to an over-angulated dog to correct a straight rear.

A novice breeder should strive to build a reputation for producing dogs that fit the standard and have few glaring faults. Some very experienced breeders might sometimes gamble by breeding to a dog with a major size or conformation fault to get another important feature they believe only that particular dog can bring to their breeding program. A beginner should avoid taking such risks until they have gained some experience with the breed. Efforts to stay within the standard will pay dividends in more consistently correct Bullmastiffs in future generations.

While a Championship title does not guarantee quality, an outstanding sire will almost invariably be awarded his Championship. Although superior dogs are easy to recognize, do not be excessively influenced by a dog's show record. A more important consideration is the quality of the offspring he sires, especially with bitches of a similar background to yours. The current reigning top dog might be a beautiful Bullmastiff, but he might not be the ideal stud for your particular bitch. If the bitch was purchased from an experienced and

Breed only the best. Ch. Dox Fast Freddy of Shady Oaks'
success in the ring is mirrored by his success as a stud dog.
(Callea Photo)

successful breeder, that person should be able to give you advice and information on the various dogs most suitable for your bitch.

NAVIGATING THE PAPERWORK

Negotiations and arrangements with the stud dog owner regarding fees, contracts and permits should have been made well before the expected date of breeding. A signed and dated contract should be provided by the stud dog owner listing the name and registration number of the dog, the stud fee, the exact terms of the contract, and whether or not a return service is offered in case the bitch does not become pregnant. Fees are determined by the owner of the stud dog and, for a proven and experienced sire, generally equal the price of a good puppy.

Read the stud contract carefully and ask questions about any point that is not clear. Clarify what constitutes a litter. If the bitch whelps one stillborn puppy, is that a litter or is a return service permitted? Identify any expenses that might be necessary in addition to the stud fee, such as veterinary costs for semen collection, artificial inseminations and shipping costs. It is a very good idea to talk with several established breeders to determine the more-or-less standard fees and conditions for your area.

Many stud dog owners require the full fee prior to the breeding, while others request a non-refundable deposit with the balance due when the litter arrives. If the fee is to be a puppy rather than cash, be very sure the terms of the choice are carefully spelled out. Also be aware that if the bitch is co-owned, you cannot promise pick of the litter to the stud owner if you have already agreed that the pick is the co-owner's option. For that matter, be certain the co-owner agrees with your choice of stud and is aware of the breeding. This saves disagreements and disappointments in the future.

COLOR CONSIDERATIONS

Brindle is a genetically dominant color pattern, while the solid red and fawn colors are recessive. This means if you wish to breed brindle puppies, at least one of the parents must be a brindle.

An ideal brindle is one whose coat is covered evenly with black stripes. The brindle may have black stripes on a fawn, red-fawn or red base color. The so-called black brindle is actually a brindle with more than 50 percent black striping on one of the solid base colors.

Since the solid colors are recessive to the brindle pattern, a pair of solid-color Bullmastiffs may only have solid-color offspring. The accepted

An ideal brindle has evenly distributed black stripes. Ch. Trojan's Dusty Warrior is a Best-in-Show winner. (Alverson)

colors come in a range of shades or tones that vary in intensity from pale silver fawn to a deep oxblood red.

The mask or muzzle color is inherited separately from the coat color, as is the ear color.

You may use coat color as one of your criteria when selecting a stud dog for your bitch, but never base your choice on color alone. The dog with the most desirable color may also be the least worthwhile in his other, more important attributes as a sire.

BREEDING YOUR BITCH

Bitches tend to have their heat cycles approximately every six months. Several weeks before coming into heat, some swelling of the vulva may become noticeable. If the bitch is to be bred, this is an indication that the stud owner should be notified that she'll be ready soon.

Watch the bitch carefully for the first sign of the bloody discharge that signals the beginning of her season. Some bitches keep themselves so clean that is possible to miss the first early days. Once the swelling becomes noticeable, wiping her vulva with a clean white tissue every morning and evening will help to inform you of first color. Once this occurs, it is your responsibility to keep her away from any possible contact with male dogs. Although you might not have a male dog of your own, your neighbors might have an intrepid, fence-climbing Don Juan who is very intent on

Never leave a bitch in season outside unattended.

secretly wooing your bitch. She should never be left unattended outside, not even in a fenced yard or garden, and she should be kept on a leash at night when out for her final constitutional before bedtime. This is a must to avoid any uninvited visitors lurking in the shadows or the shrubbery.

A bitch will normally be fertile and receptive to the male about 10 to 14 days after the start of bleeding. The discharge may turn to a pale pink or straw color at about the same time, and the vulva will soften. This phase is known as *estrus*. An experienced stud dog will often recognize this as the proper time to breed.

The bitch may indicate her readiness to be bred by presenting her rear toward the male and "flagging" her tail off to one side to invite the male to mount her. When all goes well with a natural mating, the bitch will stand steadily while the male mounts. The dog will grasp the bitch around the middle, thrust vigorously several times, deeply penetrating the vulva, and ejaculate the semen into the vagina. During this activity the glandis bulbus on the dog's penis swells, causing the two to become locked together in what is commonly called a tie. A tie can last from a few minutes to an hour or more. Do not attempt to separate a tied couple, as this can injure them both.

After the breeding, the dog, still attached to the bitch by the tie, will dismount and either stand beside her or will turn until they stand end to end, until the swelling goes down and he is released from the physical tie.

The sperm-rich part of the semen is deposited in the first few minutes of the mating, but some

These Bullmastiffs are tied. Bitches may be muzzled for safety.

seminal fluid will continue to be expressed for the duration of the tie. A tie is not absolutely necessary for a breeding to be successful, but it offers evidence that the mating was fully completed and that the semen was delivered where it was supposed to go.

It only takes one breeding to produce a litter, if it's done at the right time. However, with natural breedings the bitch is usually mated every other day for two or three matings to ensure conception.

What we've just described is how a natural breeding is *supposed* to go. Theoretically, Bullmastiffs should be able to breed on their own. But being a man-made breed, and since humans are involved in selecting the partners and choosing the dates, things do not always proceed as they should. Most experienced breeders have a collection of both humorous and hair-raising stories about breedings they conducted or heard about from someone else. It is best to have each breeding attended by someone who can assist with the mating and who can help in the event of any emergency.

When using an inexperienced stud, traveling long distances, using frozen semen or having chilled semen shipped from a distant city, we strongly recommend letting your veterinarian determine exactly when ovulation occurs. It is essential in these cases to know the exact day of ovulation to ensure the best chance for a pregnancy. Ovulation timing includes various tests that measure hormone levels, as well as the more traditional smears to check the status of cells shed from the uterine lining. These methods are often used together. You should choose a veterinarian who has experience and a proven success rate with these timing techniques. If you are using artificial insemination, do not hesitate to ask about your veterinarian's previous experience and success rate, as well.

When the American Kennel Club and the Canadian Kennel Club decided to allow the use of imported semen from foreign dogs, they enabled breeders to select from the best stud dogs available anywhere in the world. Approval must be obtained from AKC and CKC *before* a breeding using imported semen, in order to register the subsequent offspring. In addition, you need a United States Department of Agriculture permit before canine semen may be imported into the United States. Except for on-site artificial inseminations, the AKC now requires a DNA profile for all stud dogs used for extended, chilled or frozen semen breedings.

The importation of semen is still banned by the Kennel Club in Britain, but this may change in the future.

Eng. Ch. Oldwell Saxon of Bournevalley with the author, Gerry Roach. Saxon sired one of the very first litters of any breed registered with the AKC that is the product of imported semen.

TAKING CARE OF THE PREGNANT BITCH

It is often difficult to confirm a pregnancy in a Bullmastiff bitch until after the 28th day. Blood may be drawn for a hormone test at about 14 days after breeding, although a high level will not indicate whether she is pregnant or just passing through a false pregnancy. It does indicate that if pregnant, the bitch has the appropriate hormone levels to ensure a pregnancy can be held to term.

Some veterinarians can manually palpate the bitch's uterus at about 28 days and successfully tell if she is pregnant. At that stage, the uterus feels like a soft, thick rope and the developing embryos feel like hard little golf balls, lined up in a row. The period of time when these lumps are large enough to be felt and the uterus hasn't yet filled to conceal the developing puppies is very brief, so this method is not always reliable.

Ultrasound is an efficient technique to diagnose pregnancy from the fourth week, if the equipment is adequate and the practitioner experienced in this work. X-rays are frequently inconclusive until late in gestation, and by then other signs of the impending litter will become obvious. Some broadly built bitches, or those carrying small litters, may not outwardly appear to be pregnant until the final two weeks before whelping. At that time the belly will begin to distend and the breasts and mammary tissue start to enlarge.

A litter normally arrives about 63 days after the mating. This may safely vary a few days one way or the other, but before the 57th day or beyond the 68th would be cause for concern.

The pregnant bitch needs no additional supplementation with vitamins or minerals if she is eating a well-balanced, high-quality dog food. If you routinely supplement with vitamin C or folic acid, continue to do so.

Be careful not to allow the bitch to become too fat. Do not increase the amount of food until after the fourth week of pregnancy. The food then can be increased as needed to keep the bitch's ribs well covered. Sometimes, especially if the bitch is carrying a large litter or is in the later weeks of pregnancy, you may find she cannot eat as much as she normally would at each meal. If this happens, offer smaller portions and increase the number of feedings per day to compensate. Continue normal exercise in the early weeks, but curtail any strenuous activity as the pregnancy progresses.

About one week before the puppies are due, give the bitch a bath in warm water, being sure to rinse all traces of shampoo from her coat. Do not use a coat conditioner in the rinse.

PREPARING FOR THE LITTER

About a week before the litter is due, a clean, warm, dry spot should be prepared for whelping. You'll need a whelping box large enough to comfortably accommodate the bitch and her puppies. Place a blanket or towels in the bottom to encourage nesting in the chosen spot.

The whelping box may be any enclosure deep enough to prevent drafts and to contain the puppies as they grow. The sides and bottom should be easily washable. Ideally, the box will have a rail constructed around the inside approximately four inches from the floor and standing a couple of inches out from the sides (breeders call this a pig rail). This gives the pups a place to crawl and hide when their dam is rolling over, so they won't get crushed. Plastic PVC pipe, closet hanging rods, wooden dowels and two-by-two lumber all make suitable pig rails.

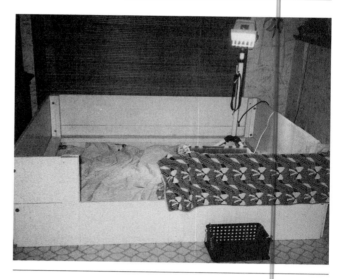

This whelping box is ready for a coming litter. Notice the railing around the inside to protect the puppies. The heat lamp will be moved outside the box when the pups arrive.

An alternative whelping box can be a large child's fiberglass or plastic wading pool. These pools are extremely easy to keep clean, but are without the extra safety of interior rails.

Newspapers should be collected for some time before the pups are due. They are used as an absorbent and disposable liner for the bottom of the whelping box. A large litter will require an incredible amount of paper to keep the whelping area clean and sanitary. Your local newspaper office may also offer roll ends of unprinted newspaper stock for sale at a low price. These roll ends are inexpensive and more cleanly handled because they have no ink on them.

Additionally, a supply of old, clean towels and washcloths should be placed near the whelping

This mom and her four-day-old pups are resting comfortably in a wading pool whelping box.

box, as well as clean bedding to replace the soiled blankets.

Place a notepad and pen where they may be easily reached to note the time of delivery, sex, weight and description of each pup. A large garbage bag or a trash can with a tight-fitting lid should be close at hand. Other items you should assemble are: a heating source, such as a waterproof heating pad or heat lamp; a thermometer; a baby scale; petroleum jelly; several boxes of facial tissues; a package of pre-moistened towelettes; rubbing alcohol; iodine; a pair of scissors; forceps; heavy sewing thread; and a small bottle of brandy.

In case of emergency, be prepared with unflavored Pedialyte and a small supply of prepared puppy formula or goat's milk. If it's necessary to replace or supplement the bitch's milk, you will need baby bottles or a French infant's feeding tube or catheter with a large syringe, depending on whether you plan to bottle feed or tube feed the puppies.

WHELPING THE LITTER

As the time approaches, the bitch's temperature will drop to slightly below 100 degrees. Sometimes this drop doesn't last long, and may be missed if her temperature is not taken several times a day. However, once it occurs, the pups will usually arrive within 24 hours.

Other signs of impending labor are restlessness, panting and a clear mucus discharge. Sometimes the bitch will refuse to eat before whelping, but this is not always a reliable clue because sometimes a bitch will eat a full meal and then immediately go to the box and give birth.

When her time approaches, alert your veterinarian and be sure to discuss what to do if there should be a problem outside of regular clinic hours. Be vigilant and do not allow the bitch outdoors unaccompanied as labor approaches. At night, take a flashlight and a small towel out with you as a precaution.

Whelping a litter is very messy work, so always wear old clothing that is expendable if it becomes permanently stained. Some breeders prefer to have their bitches whelp naturally, if they can. But the bitch will sometimes need assistance if you are to avoid losing puppies during the birthing process. She may be in mild labor for several hours before the first puppy is born, but once the contractions become visible, a puppy should arrive in short order. If she does not produce a puppy within an hour or so after hard or regular contractions begin, call the vet, as she might need to have to have a cesarean section. Waiting too long to ask for help can result in a litter of dead puppies—and in injury or death to your bitch.

If your bitch does need a C-section and you are not permitted to remain in the operating room to assist with the delivery, be sure to warn the veterinary staff never to leave your bitch alone with access to the puppies while she is recovering from the anesthesia.

A C-section is a drastic, though sometimes necessary, intervention in the birth process. But there are also other, less intrusive measures you may need to take to help your bitch and her puppies. In the womb each pup is contained in a membrane sac and attached to the placenta by the umbilical cord. During whelping this sac often breaks. At birth the dam will lick the puppy vigorously to clear away the membrane surrounding its head and face, and will crush the umbilical cord as she eats the placenta. This fairly rough treatment stimulates the pup to gasp and begin breathing on its own. If the dam does not attend to the pup, immediately clear the membrane away from the mouth and nose and encourage her to clean the puppy. If your efforts fail to get her to lick the pup, clear the mucus away from the mouth and nose area and gently rub the newborn with a soft cloth to stimulate breathing.

If that fails to revive the pup, pick it up, open the mouth with your finger, and then, while carefully supporting the head and neck, swing the pup face down in a downward arc between your legs to

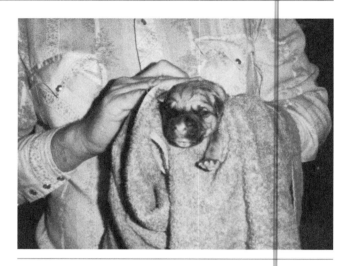

Rubbing a newborn. The pink on the nose and pads will eventually darken.

remove more fluids from the nose and chest. Massage until breathing starts. It may take up to 15 minutes to revive a pup, so be persistent in your efforts.

If the dam does not bite the umbilical cord, crush it yourself about two inches from the belly with the forceps, then cut it with the scissors and place a drop of iodine on the end of the cord. If the puppy is bleeding from the umbilical cord, re-crush the tissues with the forceps or tie off the cord with sewing thread.

With each pup, slip a finger into the mouth and feel the roof for the presence of a cleft palate, and check the body for any malformations. Any seriously defective pups should be humanely destroyed at birth. This may sound harsh, but it is more humane than letting a severely deformed animal die slowly.

Don't be shocked if some pups arrive with pink noses or footpads. They will usually turn black within the first week. Record the time of birth, sex, weight and description of the pup in your notebook. Then hold the puppy where the bitch can lick it. If there are no signs of another impending birth, lay the bitch down and place the puppy at her breast. You may need to open the puppy's mouth and place the nipple inside to encourage it to begin nursing. Make sure that each puppy nurses soon after birth to receive some colostrum from the bitch. This fluid is rich in antibodies, temporarily providing the puppies with the same immunities their dam has.

When the next pup is about to arrive, quietly remove the earlier pups to a towel-lined box that

This laboring bitch stays close to her newborns, which are in the cardboard box. This way, there is no risk of her crushing them during the next birth.

has been warmed with a hot-water bottle or heating pad. Cover the top with another towel to retain the warmth. It is essential that newborns be kept warm and never be allowed to become chilled.

Bullmastiffs tend to have large litters, so be prepared for a long night of whelping. When all the pups are born, take the bitch outdoors to relieve her bladder and then offer her some milk with a couple of egg yolks beaten into it. She may be reluctant to leave the pups, so keep a leash handy to remove her from the area. Clean the box while she is out, replacing the bedding with a layer of clean papers and a fresh blanket. Wash and towel dry the dam's hindquarters before returning her to the nest.

It is important that you account for each placenta as the pups are born, because a retained placenta may cause serious health problems for the bitch. Identical twins sharing a single placenta are quite rare in Bullmastiffs, so if one is missing, mention it to the vet when he or she checks the bitch later.

Have the veterinarian examine both mother and pups. He may give her an injection to cause her to strongly contract and expel any material still remaining in the uterus. This also often helps to stimulate the production of milk. The bitch will continue to have a discharge for the next few days, so do not let her into sections of the house where the dark fluid can cause permanent stains.

Occasionally a bitch will appear to reject her pups at first. Encourage her to care for them, but if she growls or shows any aggressive behavior toward them, take it as a serious warning. She may settle down in a day or two and become an excellent mother, but in the meantime take every precaution with the litter to avoid any possible disaster. She should be removed and only returned to the box to nurse when she is muzzled or there are adequate hands to comfortably restrain her, if necessary. A wire-mesh exercise pen around the nest will allow her to see and hear the pups, yet prevent her from doing any damage.

As a general rule, we *never* leave our puppies unattended with the bitch during the first three weeks of life. Even a good and caring mother can roll over and inadvertently smother or crush a tiny puppy without realizing it. It's up to you to decide if you want to take that risk.

In the days after whelping, watch the bitch for any complications. If she should suddenly show abnormal behavior or bouts of shivering, she might be suffering from a serious condition called eclampsia, which is caused by a sharp drop in calcium in the bloodstream. Contact the vet immediately. The condition can usually be easily remedied with a calcium injection.

Examine the nipples daily to be sure there is an adequate flow of milk and that there is no redness, swelling or heat, which would indicate mastitis.

REARING THE LITTER

Healthy newborn Bullmastiff pups are usually a contented and fairly quiet bunch. Except for those affected by the anesthesia from a cesarean birth, any persistent or unexplained crying should be considered an indication of trouble. The pup could be cold, not getting enough to eat or suffering from some defect or illness.

Do not be in a great hurry to give the pups any formula or supplemental feedings in the first 24 to 36 hours.

Watch for the presence of activated sleep. Normal healthy puppies tend to twitch and jerk several times a minute while whey are asleep. One of the earliest and most subtle signs of fading puppies in the first week is the lack of this activated sleep.

Weigh each pup at the same time each day, and record the weight in your notebook for comparison. They should gain at a steady rate. Also periodically check for any sign of dehydration by gently

Ch. Licassa Delightful Lady of Oldwell is busy nursing her litter. Note the PVC pipe railing around the inside of the whelping box.

pinching the skin at the scruff of the neck between your fingers and pulling slightly upward. When released, the skin should immediately slide back into place. If it remains peaked more than a few seconds, it is an indication of dehydration and additional fluids are probably needed. If you are concerned that the pups might need extra fluids, give them unflavored Pedialyte or a glucose solution recommended by your veterinarian.

When handling the puppies, be sure to look at their eyes, too. If the unopened eyes appear to be swollen or bulging, take the puppy to your veterinarian immediately. An infection under the eyelid could destroy the eye, and it must be opened to drain.

These newborns are sleeping in a loose pile on a blanket, indicating that the environment is comfortably warm.

Newborn puppies are not able to regulate their body temperature, and must be kept in approximately an 85-degree environment for the first weeks of life. Once the pups are up on their feet and able to walk, the temperature may be gradually lowered to 70 degrees. Place a folded blanket in the center of the whelping box with a waterproof heating pad beneath it on the lowest setting. A heat lamp suspended over the middle of the box offers a gentle, radiant type of warmth. When the temperature is just right, the pups will gather in a loose pile on the blanket and sleep with little fussing. If they're too hot, they will leave the blanket and sprawl on the papers around the perimeter. If they are too cold, they will tend to cry and mound together in a restless, tightly packed mound.

Just as chilling is a serious problem, do not allow the pups to be overheated. Adjust the heat

sources to gain the optimum temperature of about 85 degrees and to keep the litter in relative comfort. Placing the bedding and heat source in the center of the box serves several purposes: It draws the pups together into the middle where the bitch is less apt to step on them or lay down on one. The bitch consequently rests on the unheated edge of the blanket curling around the pups, and remains comfortable and not affected by the extra heat the little ones require. It also gives the pups a cooler place to crawl away to, if their hot spot is just too hot.

Newborn puppies cannot urinate or defecate on their own. They require stimulation to initiate elimination. An experienced mother will usually take care of this by licking the puppy's anal region. But Bullmastiff bitches are sometimes reluctant to clean their puppies, particularly those experiencing motherhood for the first time. The instinct to lick and clean the puppies may be encouraged by inducing the puppy's urine flow while holding the puppy above the bitch's muzzle. Use a cotton ball that has been dipped in warm water to gently massage the area.

If the dam refuses to clean the pups, you must do it for her. If this is not done, fecal matter may cake under the tail, sometimes completely sealing off the anal area. To avoid this problem, apply a lubricant such as baby oil or petroleum jelly under the tail area, and then gently massage the pup with a soft tissue until it fully relieves itself several times a day. If you are supplementing or hand feeding the pups, do this every time they are fed.

Wiping with a damp cloth cleans the puppy and accustoms it to being handled. A disposable moist towelette can be used to induce elimination.

Occasionally a bitch will not have enough milk to feed a large litter, and in some instances she will have no milk at all. In that case, the breeder must feed the puppies. This may be done either with a baby bottle or by tube feeding. A bottle for one or two puppies is no problem, but with a large, fully hand-fed litter, you'll barely have finished feeding, cleaning and burping each pup before it's time to start all over again!

If you're using a bottle, select a nipple that allows only a moderate rate of flow. Too much formula given too rapidly can choke a pup, and puts it at risk for aspiration pneumonia from inhaling the fluid into its lungs. Each pup should also be burped by gently patting and rubbing the back after bottle-fed meals.

Once breeders master the technique of tube feeding, they rarely use a baby bottle again. It involves inserting a plastic tube down the newborn's esophagus and gently letting formula flow directly into the stomach. Obviously, this is a delicate procedure. Your veterinarian or an experienced breeder can teach you the proper way to tube feed.

There are a number of commercial puppy formulas on the market. Fresh goat's milk or diluted evaporated goat's milk is also an excellent substitute, especially for litters that are only being supplemented. It does not have the exact fat and protein content of bitch's milk, but it is close enough. The naturally homogenized fat in goat's milk is easy for the puppies to digest and they will thrive on it. Fresh or evaporated cow's milk is a poor choice, and should be avoided.

The newborn puppy that is fully hand raised requires at least 60 to 70 calories per pound of body weight each day. Its nutritional requirements increase by about 10 calories per pound each week, through the fourth week. Calculate the total amount the puppy needs each day and divide that into four meals.

A puppy that is nursing and receiving some milk from its dam is merely being supplemented, so be careful not to over-feed. Your goal should be to keep the puppies alive and thriving until they are old enough to eat on their own.

The eyes open between the 10th and 14th day, but vision does not become clear until the third week. From the 21st day onward, the puppies experience a great sensory awakening. Suddenly they can see and hear. They begin more orga-nized play, notice toys and items placed in their box, recognize individuals and start the long process of learning. Pups are coordinated enough to learn to lap up liquids from a shallow bowl, and thus begin the weaning process.

Learning to eat can be a messy proposition. The pups should be thoroughly cleaned with a warm, wet cloth after every meal. Be sure to wipe the entire head and chest area, and don't forget to wash the feet, including between the toes.

As they grow, the puppies will need more and more space. Keeping the whelping box clean becomes a tremendous effort, especially if the litter is a large one. Once on solid food at about four weeks of age, we move the pups from the original whelping box to a rectangular pen. Puppies begin to leave the nest to relieve themselves as soon as

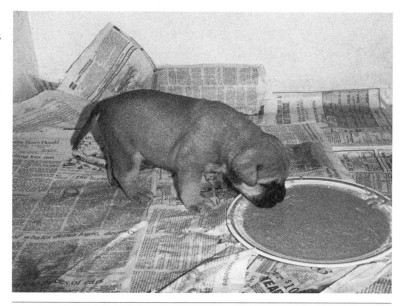

Start weaning to soft food from a shallow dish.

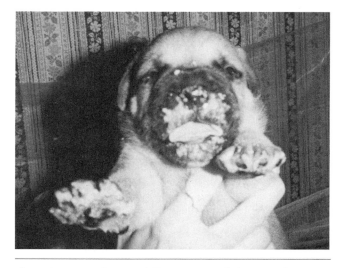

Learning to eat is messy! Be sure to wash between the toes, too.

they can control their own bodily func-
tions. The new pen capitalizes on that
innate sense of cleanliness by dividing the
area into two distinct sections. In one area
the pups have a blanket and a continued
source of warmth, such as the overhead
lamp. The other, larger section is carpeted
with layers of flat newspaper, and on top
of that are several inches of finely shredded paper. The toys are placed in this part
of the pen and the puppies soon play
riotously, racing through the shred. They
also learn to relieve themselves in the
shred, and the deep fluffy paper keeps any
feces from coming in direct contact with
the pups. Make sure to scoop and replace
this paper very frequently.

*When a larger pen is needed, divide it into sleeping and eating space at
one end, and shredded paper at the other.*

When the litter is six to seven weeks
old, we start to separate the pups into smaller
groups or pairs and get them accustomed to sleeping in crates. This also serves as preliminary housebreaking. The crates are placed near a door, and as
soon as the puppies are released, they are immediately hurried directly outdoors to relieve themselves. It is essential that someone accompany them
to be sure that each and every pup urinates and
defecates before the group returns inside. Many
pups that have been raised this way require very
little further housebreaking. This is successful, however, only if you are diligent about taking pups
outdoors often enough to prevent accidents from
becoming commonplace in the crate. If the litter
must spend long hours unattended, it would be
better to leave them in the pen.

The initial worming is usually done at three to
four weeks with a palatable and safe product such
as Evict or Nemex (pyrantal pamoate). If the dam
has ever had roundworms or you have a multiple-
dog household, do not wait until a fecal exam
shows eggs in the sample before worming. By
then, the pups have developed a mature worm
population and have already shed infectious worm
eggs into their environment or reinfested the
mother. The process can be repeated at three- to
four-week intervals, especially if parasites are
observed in the stools following the worming.

Your veterinarian will recommend an inoculation sequence. Usually one to two combination
injections are given to each puppy before it leaves
for its new home.

Puppies are a legacy for the future

The litter registration application should have been sent to the AKC (or other appropriate kennel club) shortly after birth to ensure that the individual registration papers will arrive before the litter's departure.

Each puppy should be tattooed on the groin area with its individual AKC registration number, found on the blue slip. The procedure is not painful and they tolerate this very well at about seven weeks of age. Over the years, we have discovered that a good, legible puppy tattoo rarely needs to be retouched at adulthood. When possible, the litter should also be microchipped and listed with a registry. A microchip is a tiny transmitter, about the size of a grain of rice, that is inserted under the dog's skin. It is then read with a scanner. Microchips must be placed by a veterinarian, who can give you more information. The AKC has a microchip registry service.

It is your responsibility as a breeder to carefully screen all potential homes for your puppies, prepare all paperwork, keep accurate records, place pet-quality pups where they will not be used for breeding, always be available for assistance and information, and give each puppy in the litter the absolute best possible start in life.

CHAPTER 11

The British Scene

M any of the founders of our breed also bred Mastiffs, and many Mastiff breeders also bred Bullmastiffs. Some of these breeders registered littermates, one as a Mastiff and one as a Bullmastiff. The Kennel Club in Britain seemed to operate under a policy whereby if the dog looked like a certain breed and its breeder said it was that breed, the KC would register it as that breed. It sometimes appears that puppies were sold as Mastiffs or Bullmastiffs, according to the demand of the moment. In August 1921, the KC registered Poor Jerry, sired by Poor Joe out of Peggy, as a Mastiff. The same KC had, that very April, registered Sir Roger as a Bullmastiff—sired by Poor Joe out of Peggy.

Because some of these early breeders were hardly of sterling character, and since the registration policies of the Kennel Club were obviously lax, the formative years of the breed are murky indeed.

THE CIRCLE OF THREE

Samuel Moseley, who was a key figure in garnering Kennel Club recognition for Bullmastiffs, continued to be very active in the breed after recognition. His Hamil, and later Farcroft Kennels, were the foundations of the breed. This is not to say that other early breeders, such as J. D. Biggs (Osmaston Kennel) and Doris Mullins (Mulorna Kennel) did not make serious contributions. However, Moseley was the first great builder, by virtue of the sheer numbers of dogs produced. A review in the *Town and Country News* in July 1925 reported that Moseley had five stud dogs and 16 brood bitches at his kennels. It also said more than 100 puppies were bred a year. If, indeed, he kept 16 brood bitches, it is possible they produced that many puppies in a year.

Farcroft Felons Frayeur, one of Moseley's early registered Bullmastiffs.

Ch. Tiger Prince, a cornerstone of the breed.

Farcroft dogs were used to some degree by most other breeders in forming their own lines. Victor J. Smith (Pridzor Kennel) and Jack Barnard (Paddington Kennel) were Moseley's strongest competitors in these early years. The first Challenge Certificates for the breed were offered at Crufts in 1928, and were won by Smith's Tiger Prince (Tiger Torus out of Princess Poppy) and Moseley's Farcroft Silvo (Hamil Grip out of Farcroft Belltong).

These three men—Moseley, Smith and Barnard—as owners and breeders accounted for seven of the eight Challenge Certificates available in 1928; all 10 CCs in 1929; 11 of the 12 in 1930; 10 of the 14 in 1931; and eight of the 18 offered in 1932. By that year, other breeders had caught up

and competition became fierce. Moseley managed one more CC in 1933 with his bitch Farcroft Fragment (Ch. Farcroft Finality out of Ch. Farcroft Silvo). He also bred Margaret Rose's bitch CC winner in 1936, Rosland Felice (Farcroft Formative out of Farcroft Staunch). His career was basically over, but he had a terrific run.

Barnard co-bred with Mullins, and the dog that resulted, Ch. Tenz (Vindictive Prince out of Princess Ursula), won two CCs in 1934. However, like Moseley, his dominance in the show ring was at an end. Mullins, who acquired her first Bullmastiff in 1926 (the year before purebred status), went on to establish a strain that gave the name Mulorna Red to the lovely oxblood mahogany color that is so rare nowadays.

Victor Smith continued with his Pridzor dogs into the early 1950s, but had to share the winning with the newer upcoming breeders.

Marcus of Mulorna, one of Doris Mullins' early dogs.

THE NEXT WAVE

The next wave of breeders, building on the work of the early pioneers, produced some dogs whose names ring down through Bullmastiff history. The box on page 126 lists some of them. All were famous dogs in their day, and most played major roles in firmly establishing the breed as purebred.

Ch. Jeanette of Brooklands won two CCs, the last at the Kennel Club Show in 1935. She was sold by Spruce to John W. Cross of the United States, and you'll read more about her in Chapter 12.

There were many other breeders who must also receive credit for playing a part in the early furtherance of the breed. E. Burton and his Navigation Bullmastiffs are among the notables. The Wooloowin dogs of the pre-teen Miss J. Howe of Avaston, Derby, were quite well-known and are advertised in Craven's first edition of 1932. In the same book, Mrs. J. Murray-Smith of London and Capt. C. Traill, MC, of Berkshire, shared a page advertising Ch. Athos, Castlehill Rajah, Ch. Castlehill Peggy Ann, Lady Goo Goo and Noble.

Frances and Ted Warren became enamored of the breed in 1929, only four short years after KC recognition. They adopted Harbex as a prefix—a name that would become synonymous with the brindle color. This is ironic, in a way, as the Bullmastiff that first sparked their interest in the breed was a fawn. In an article published in *The Welsh and West of England Bullmastiff Society Silver Jubilee Supplement,* Frances said she and Ted waited two years, unsuccessfully trying to obtain a fawn dog. Giving up, they settled for a brindle, and eventually made breed history by winning the first Challenge Certificate taken by a brindle dog with their Peregrine of Harbex. Later on, more history was made when their Chips of Harbex, in 1951, became the first brindle Champion dog in Britain.

Prizdor Warrior, a 1940s dog from Victor Smith.

EARLY BRITISH NOTABLES

Ch. Athos (Farcroft Fidelity out of Noble), bred by Mrs. J. Murray Smith

Ch. Roger of the Fenns (Don Juan out of Luzlow Princess), bred by D. F. Wedgewood and owned by J. Toney (The Fenns Kennel)

Ch. Peter of the Fenns (Farcroft Formative out of Farcroft Staunch), bred by Samuel Moseley and owned by J. Toney

Ch. Sans Faute (Buller's Fidelity out of Wingate's Pride), owned by W. Crumblehulme and bred by George Bullough (who bragged in his advertisements, "Not only do I breed winning specimens, but sell winners")

Ch. Simba (Athos out of Lady Athena), bred by G. Pollard and owned by Lord Londonderry

Ch. Bubbles (Farcroft Felon's Frayeur out of Lady Betty of Bowdencourt), bred by D. Hardman and owned by Tom Pennington (Bartonville Kennel)

Ch. Wendy of Bulmas (Peter of the Fenns out of Sheila of Bulmas), bred and owned by Cyril Leeke and Mrs. G. Hill (Bulmas Kennel)

The Stanfell dogs of Mr. and Mrs. J. Higginson

Eng./Am. Ch. Jeanette of Brooklands (Ch. Roger of the Fenns out of Ch. Bubbles), bred by T. Pennington and owned by E. L. Spruce

It is interesting that among the high points of her 40-year career, Frances Warren mentions winning a trophy for "dog or bitch with strongest muzzle allied to a level mouth" with a bitch from the Bulmas Kennel that she bought from Cyril Leeke in the 1930s. Modern breeders who would change the breed standard to prefer an undershot mouth should be aware that they would discard decades of work by breeders such as the Warrens.

The Warrens of Harbex are also noteworthy in that they saved the brindle color for the breed after World War II. Frances writes in her article, "In 1950 we were back to our full quota of 15 dogs and bitches, and, because during the war the brindles had almost completely died out again, we determined to concentrate on them. Our old Big Bill was past use and after much searching we discovered a dog, bred before the war, who had never seen a bitch in his seven years. He was bred by Miss Nesfield, by Grimm of Harbex out of Chloe of Harbex (brindle), registered Highland Laddie. It took us nine hours to get a mating with Harbex Jane, but from that, and one subsequent litter, have stemmed all the brindles in the world today." Every Bullmastiff fancier that admires the brindle color owes the Warrens a tremendous debt of gratitude.

CYRIL LEEKE AND BULMAS

The next giant was Cyril Leeke. He and Mrs. Hill originated the Bulmas Kennels in 1929. Bulmas was at the forefront among Bullmastiff kennels in

CRAVEN'S HEADLINERS

Arthur Craven's book, *The Bull Mastiff as I Know It*, was the first written on the breed. It contained many advertisements for kennels that today we recognize as great contributors to the breed. They include:

H. Barron, (Barron's Kennel)
Charles Froggatt (Westhoughton Kennel)
S. E. Moseley (Farcroft Kennel)
George Bullough (Bullough's Kennel)
Miss Jane Lane in Sussex
The Kenwood Kennel at Manchester
Mr. and Mrs. E. Bury (Timberdine Kennel)
A. Fraser (Lohaire Kennel)
W. Crumblehulme
M.P.S of Lancashire
J. Heaton (Heaton's Kennel)
T. Pennington (Bartonville Kennel), featuring
    Pridzor King
Jack Barnard, featuring Tiger Vindictive and
    Vindictive Prince

In Craven's second edition, published in 1937, we find:

Tiger Vindictive and Vindictive Prince.

Arthur Pennington (Arpens Kennel),
    featuring Arpens Golden Lion
Dr. T. Wilson Shaw, Rodenhurst, featuring
    Rodenhurst Rajah
Frances A. Warren (Harbex Kennel)

the 1940s and early '50s. Leeke, Hill and later Mary Barker are credited with establishing a modern type that became so popular that other breeders were forced to follow.

Sheila of Bulmas (Rusty Rufus out of Tara), bred to Ch. Peter of the Fenns (Farcroft Formative out of Farcroft Staunch), produced Ch. Wendy of Bulmas, the first Bulmas champion. Wendy was

bred to Ch. Roger of the Fenns (Don Juan out of Luzlow Princess) and, with her whelps, Champions Billy and Beppo, Bulmas Kennel was off and running. Like Farcroft, every Bullmastiff line has a Bulmas somewhere in the pedigree.

Bulmas continued its influence until 1957, when Leeke, then in partnership with Barker, immigrated to the United States to take up

Cyril Leeke, shown with one of his early dogs, is often considered the founder of modern Bullmastiff type.

eventually severed his connections with the breed. He died in 1971.

RODENHURST KENNEL

The Rodenhurst prefix was first used by Dr. T. Wilson Shaw on Rodenhurst Susanne and Rodenhurst Rajah. It was later taken up by E. L. Spruce, who had allowed his Brooklands prefix to

Ch. Branch of Bulmas, considered one of the best of Leeke's stud dogs.

employment with R. Lee Twitty, of Twit-Lee Bullmastiffs. Leeke took some of the best dogs and bitches in Britain with him to the U.S. We'll look at what effect this had on the dogs bred on the East Coast of the United States in Chapter 12.

Leeke had been cautioned against this move by his old friend Leonard V. Smith (Bullmast Kennel), who was then living in California. Smith had immigrated to the United States in 1951, and, with his daughter Patricia, was quite active in the breed. True to Smith's predictions, the association with Twitty was not a happy one, and Leeke and Barker returned to Britain in 1960. That, unfortunately, was the end of Bulmas. Leeke retired and lapse during the war years. We have been unable to find any connection between Shaw and Spruce, although one may have existed. In any case, in 1949 Spruce bred a dog that has had perhaps more influence on the North American scene than any other. This was the great Ch. Rodenhurst Masterpiece (Rodenhurst Duke out of Tasmar Daffodil). Probably every Bullmastiff breeding program active today in the United States and Canada has Masterpiece in its pedigrees, primarily through two of his famous sons, Ch. Rodenhurst Marksman and Ch. Ambassador of Buttonoak, or his daughter Rodenhurst Maisie.

Marksman's blood was of great influence in Canada and on the West Coast of the United States. Yasmin of Glamview was imported while in whelp to Ambassador, and the litter directly influenced American breeding. Maisie's impact was felt mostly in the Midwest through imports, which contained the blood of her matings with Ch. Goodstock Lord Joyful. Spruce retired from dogs in the early 1950s—a great loss to the breed.

BUTTONOAK AND THE OTHER PLAYERS

The next major player on the scene was the Buttonoak Kennel of E. L. Terry. Buttonoak was basically two lines. First was the Bulmas type, with heavier bone and harsher coat, as represented by Ch. Antony of Buttonoak (Bulmas Marco of Lisvane out of Ch. Bimbi of Bulmas), whelped in 1951. The other was a new type, cleaner in outline with the modern shorter, sleeker coat represented by Ch. Ambassador of

Buttonoak (Ch. Rodenhurst Masterpiece out of Ch. Swatchway Amethyst of Buttonoak), whelped in 1953.

Marco and Bimbi, Antony's sire and dam, were mostly Bulmas and Stanfell, while Masterpiece and Amethyst, Ambassador's sire and dam, had some Bulmas and Stanfell blood (few dogs did not by this time) but also went back to other dogs that were not as heavily used by Leeke in forming his Bulmas line, such as the Mulorna dog Rhodian.

Ch. Almericus of Buttonoak, who came to the United States, was one of the great dogs, bred by combining the Ambassador and Antony lines.

Ruth Short's Bulstaff Kennel combined these two Buttonoak lines to produce the all-time top CC-winning Bullmastiff in Britain, the great Ch. Bulstaff Achilles. Short's influence on the American as well as the British scene was all out of proportion to the number of dogs she bred.

Ch. Ambassador of Buttonoak is behind many of the great Bullmastiffs in the world today. (Wyant)

Buttonoak, combined with Mrs. Millard's Marbette line, was the foundation stock of the now world-famous Oldwell Kennels, which holds the record for having bred and owned the most British Champions in breed history.

THE MODERN ERA IN BRITAIN

As the 1950s came to a close, there were other significant breeders. Granville and Doreen Blount of Naukeen Kennels came into the breed, and both became noted and popular judges. One of their well-known dogs, which won Best of Breed at Crufts in 1971, was Ch. Stephan of Naukeen (Ch. Claude of Oldwell out of Samantha of Naukeen). The Blounts have exported their Naukeen dogs around the world, including the United States.

Margaret Reynolds' Yorkist Kennel was known for beautiful black-masked, silver fawns, and produced Champions that were used in many breeding programs.

Walter and Lyn Pratt of Kelwall Kennels became interested in the Bullmastiff in 1954. They eventually acquired their first in 1957, Aaliz of Buttonoak (Marcus of Lisvane out of Bulways Brumas). Ch. Frederick of Kelwall (Ch. Showell Yibor out of Ebony of Kelwall) won Best of Breed at Crufts and was Dog of the Year. Another well-known Kelwall Bullmastiff was Ch. Bonnie of Kelwall, sired by Azer of Oldwell out of Ailsa of Kelwall. A daughter of Frederick and Bonnie, Cluny of Kelwall would become the foundation bitch of Bill Walkey's Shayla Kennels in British Columbia, Canada. Lyn also became another of the

Ch. Claude of Oldwell, a modern type Bullmastiff.

breed's great historians and writers, and took up the mantle of Frances Warren, working to keep the flame burning for brindles.

The Goodhall sisters' Goodstock Bullmastiffs were influential both in Britain and the United States. Their famous Ch. Goodstock Lord Joyful (Goodstock Teddy of Lowston out of Queen of Stockport) was widely used.

Jim and Dorothy Price's Lombardy prefix is known worldwide. Lombardy Kennels was started in 1950 with a bitch, Braid of Bulmas, sired by the famous Ch. Branch of Bulmas out of Bright Eyes of Bulmas. Other purchases followed, and success as breeders was not far behind. The first Lombardy champion, Ch. Harvester of Lombardy (Marci of Lombardy out of Gimingham No Trumps), is perhaps the best known and was widely used. The Prices are well-known judges, and Dorothy has judged in North America.

Douglas Oliff and his Wyaston Kennel came into the breed around 1947 and eventually became one of its icons, through his writing and judging in the United Kingdom and the United States. He wrote *The Mastiff and Bullmastiff Handbook*. He judged the American Bullmastiff Association Golden Jubilee National Specialty in the United States, and returned to judge at a subsequent National Specialty Show in 1988. He became a member of the Welsh Bullmastiff Society in 1949, became its secretary in 1956 and served in that post for 28 years. He was instrumental in changing the area served by that society to include the West Country of England. This very astute move helped ensure the club's survival.

Oliff's vision of Bullmastiffs sometimes differed from that of some of his contemporaries, and not being a large breeder, he cannot count as many Champions as some. He prefers a more substantial dog with a powerful, bully head. This preference was reflected in his judging choices in American specialties. Perhaps his most influential dog was Wyaston Captain Cuttle. One of that dog's daughters out of Wyaston Elizabeth Tudor was Wyaston Lady Hamilton. She was the dam of Ch. Bulstaff Argus of Arancrag, a dog that was extremely

influential in America, especially through the Scyldocga Kennels.

Gerald and Doris Warren of Copperfield Kennel (no relation to the Harbex Warrens) are another influential breeding duo. Gerald was reared by his grandfather, a gamekeeper. The grandfather kept crossbred Bullmastiffs—working Night Dogs. This was Gerald's introduction to the breed to which he later became so devoted.

He began his career in 1947 with the bitch Lady Deborah and produced many outstanding Bullmastiffs. Gerald stated he has bred an average of 15 to 20 litters. Perhaps the best-known result was Ch. Copperfield Sarah Pocket, who won 11 of the 13 Challenge Certificates in her sex offered in one year.

In 1966 Gerald married Doris, who quickly became a breeder in her own right. Doris has bred about 70 litters since their marriage. Copperfield will be well tended for some time by their son

Gerald Warren in a 1940s snapshot with one of his Copperfield dogs.

Billy Warren, who is quite rightly a Bullmastiff fancier, judge and breeder, as well.

Copperfield's best-known stud dog was actually an Oldwell dog that Gerald bought in 1973 named Maverick of Copperfield of Oldwell. Maverick was sired by Ch. Regent of Oldwell out of Ch. Oldwell Queen Guenivere of Mureken. He won one Challenge Certificate and two Reserves. He went on to sire 90 litters, which included 30 Champions around the world.

The name Oldwell is recognized the world over by knowledgeable Bullmastiff fanciers. Like Farcroft, Bulmas, Buttonoak and Bulstaff, Harry and Beryl Colliass's Oldwell Kennel was a major influence indeed. Their first Bullmastiff, Reckless Roger, was acquired as a pet in 1935. Finding no fault in the breed as companion and watch dog, Harry and Beryl looked for a replacement upon Roger's natural demise in 1942. They were unable to find another dog, and finally bought a bitch named Benign of Bulmas. Later a second bitch, Brown Bairn of Bulmas, was purchased from Cyril Leeke.

Both bitches were bred, but the offspring were not quite what they were looking for. Harry and Beryl saw some of the qualities they wanted in the Marbette line, and other qualities on the Ambassador side of the Buttonoak line. A bitch, May Queen of Marbette, was purchased from Millard. May Queen was bred to Ace of Buttonoak, a litter brother to Ambassador.

From this breeding came the first of the great Oldwell Champions, Ch. Bambino, who won a Best of Breed at Crufts over Ambassador. Millard promptly took a litter sister of May Queen, Ch. Mi-Choice of Marbette, to Ambassador. This mating produced Ch. Mi-Brandy of Marbette and Ch. Oldwell Mi-Trooper of Marbette. From these matings came the start of the Oldwell dogs that would just about dominate the British show ring in the 1970s and 1980s, and still must be considered a strong force in the 1990s. Harry and Beryl are in their late 80s as this book is written, but they continue with the assistance of their daughter Ann Colliass and their associate, Billy Brittle. In Britain, few modern pedigrees do not have an Oldwell in them. In the United States and Canada, the blood of Ch. Rowley of Oldwell and the brindle

Billy Warren at age four with Ch. Copperfield Martin Chuzzlewit.

half-brothers Sambo of Oldwell and Ch. Securus Erebus are to be found in many of the winning kennels.

Many other fanciers have contributed much to the British scene. Some of them are listed in the box on pages 136–137. Perhaps one of these kennels will assume the dominant position once held by the great kennels of Farcroft, Bulmas, Buttonoak, Bulstaff and Oldwell. The future in Britain looks interesting indeed.

THE BRITISH SHOW SCENE

There is no national or parent club to oversee the Bullmastiff in the United Kingdom. Instead, Bullmastiffs are represented by five Championship Clubs serving different areas of the country: The British Bullmastiff League, The Southern Bullmastiff Society, The Welsh and West of England, The Bullmastiff Association and The Northern Bullmastiff Club. The five clubs are loosely affiliated in

Ace of Buttonoak, a foundation sire of the Oldwell Kennel.

Harry Colliass with Ch. Honeybee of Oldwell. She represents the distinctive Oldwell look.

an organization called the Breed Council, but its powers are limited. The Scottish Bullmastiff Club represents the breed in Scotland.

Championships are not gained the way they are in North America. Instead, the Kennel Club allocates a limited number of sets of Challenge Certificates per breed each year, with an equal number for each sex. They are divided among the all-breed and single-breed clubs. This division is done arbitrarily, and there is no guarantee that all the single-breed clubs will receive a set of Challenge Certificates.

A dog or bitch is required to win three Challenge Certificates under three different judges to be awarded the title of Champion. Four sets of Challenge Certificates were allocated in 1928. Twenty-seven sets are currently offered.

In Great Britain, Champions of record compete in the Open Class for their sex. The other classes are:

- Minor Puppy—dogs six to nine months old

- Puppy—dogs of six to 12 months old

- Junior—dogs of six to 18 months old

- Post-Graduate—dogs that have not won a CC or five or more first prizes at Championship Shows in Post-Graduate, Minor Limit, Mid-Limit, Limit or Open Classes

- Limit—dogs that have not won three CCs under three different judges or seven or more first prizes in all at Championship Shows in Limit and Open Classes

- Open—all dogs of the breed for which the class is provided

These classes are divided by sex. Other classes that may be offered whenever a large entry is expected are Maiden, Novice, Debutante, Graduate, Tyro and Mid-Limit.

This Oldwell puppy recently made her debut in the show ring, carrying on a long tradition. (Carol Ann Johnson)

THE RECORD HOLDERS

The record holders for numbers of CCs won as of 1997 are the Short's Ch. Bulstaff Achilles, a dog (Ch. Bulstaff Brobdingnag out of Ch. Bulstaff Ambssadress of Buttonoak), who won 24 Challenge Certificates; and Jackie Ling's Ch. Dajean Goldust the Poachersfoe, a bitch (Ch. Saturn of Graecia out of Dajean Golden Autocrat), who won 21 Challenge Certificates.

Ch. Dixson of the Green (Ch. Norwegian Wood of Rodekes out of Lady Chameleon), a dog bred and owned by Edward Thompson, is so far the only Bullmastiff to win more than one all-breed Best in Show in Britain. His Best in Show at the South Wales Kennel Club Show was the first for the breed in the United Kingdom in 45 years.

Ch. Bulstaff Achilles on the left. His progeny were of great influence in the United States. That's Ch. Little Miss of Oldwell on the right. (Cooke)

Ch. Norwegian Wood of Rodekes, the sire of Ch. Dixon of the Green. Dixon is the only Bullmastiff to win more than one British all-breed Best in Show.

MODERN HEADLINERS

Jim and Ethyl Leeson and their son Michael (Pitman's Kennel) made quite a splash, winning the Centennial Show with their Ch. Pitman's Gentleman Jim. A few years later they also brought out the impressive Ch. Sharwell's Mean Mr. Mustard of Pitmans.

Edna Evans (Seafoam Kennel), a member of the Kennel Club, bred Ch. Seafoam Miranda. Her expertise is quite in demand as a Championship-level judge in the United Kingdom, Australia, New Zealand and the United States.

Bill and Jan Newton came into the breed in 1970, first under the Craigylea banner. Their dog, Ch. Craigylea's Sir Galahad, won the Working Group at Crufts. The Newtons inadvertently allowed the prefix Craigylea to lapse and had to choose another name. They selected Galastock, and promptly produced a dog almost as famous as Galahad in their Ch. Galastock's Danny Boy.

Mary Cox (Colom Kennel) started in the 1960s with stock from the Lombardy line. Perhaps her best-known Bullmastiff is the bitch Ch. Colom Florin (Ch. Lombardy Simon of Silverfarm out of Lombardy Rosamunda). Colom has exported Bullmastiffs all over Europe and North America.

Bill and Fran Harris (Bunsoro Kennel) began in Bullmastiffs in 1968 and have since made their mark upon the breed. Their latest, Ch. Bunsoro Red Sails, is an outstanding specimen. Bunsoro also furnished the beginnings of Tom and Dorothy Massey's Todomas prefix, as well as Malcolm and Angela McInnes' Morvern prefix. Bill Walkey (Shayla Kennel) imported Bunsoro dogs to Canada.

Ch. Saturn of Graecia (Ch. Graecia Centaur out of Wilward Naughty Nina) and Ch. Graecia Mercury (Saturn out of Graecia Gemini) are two fine examples of the breeding program of Alan and Mave Rostron (Graecia Kennel).

Alex and Janet Gunn (Flintstock Kennel) won Best of Breed at Crufts in 1992 with their outstanding bitch Ch. Lepsco Lady Elise of Flintstock. John and Sue Reynolds (Tartuffe Kennel) maintain a large kennel and have produced several fine champions.

Derek and Rose Higginson and Derek Jr. (Rodeke Kennel) quickly found success with Ch. Norwiegan Wood of Rodeke. They are establishing their breeding program with Oldwell and Pitmans dogs.

Julie Jones (Jobull Kennel) is breeding a combination of Pitmans, combined with vom Frankenthal dogs from

Ch. Bunsoro Bombardier was Top Stud Dog in 1981.

Germany. She imported Blazin's Jubullation of Jobull from the United States and finished her British championship.

Messrs. Blunden and Quantrill, (Licassa Kennel) have produced several champions, including Ch. Licassa Jolly Roger and the three sisters, Ch. Licassa Lady Clara of Oldwell, Ch. Licassa Little Diamond and Am. Ch. Licassa Delightful Lady of Oldwell. The sisters are from a mating between Ch. Oldwell Trumps and Licassa Lady Rogina.

Other well-known breeders today include:

The Filers (Barrus Kennel)
John and Muriel Bisatt (Murbisa Kennel)
The Bullocks (Bullenca Kennel)
Clara Risdale (Wyburn Kennel)
The Clements (Wraxallvale Kennel)
V. I. Cole (Phirene Kennel)
M. Tonge (Tanglehill Kennel)
The Wrays (Voncalin Kennel)
Daphne Pegler and Felicity Wilson
   (Cadenham Kennel)
The Jameses (Jamemos Kennel)
Ewart and Sally Grant (Jagofpeeko Kennel)
Colin and Mary Jones (Maxstoke Kennel)
Fiona Miller (Meitza Kennel)
Shelley Tomsett (Dajean Kennel)
Linda Wade (Patchings Kennel)
Jackie Ling (Poachersfoe Kennel)
Duncan and Anne Bowman (Bournevalley
   Kennel)
Grant Slater (Chalfs), owner of the famous
   Ch. Dajean Red Dragon

Bunsoro Red Molly is a nice red bitch.

Ch. Dajean Red Dragon, one the breed's great show dogs.

CHAPTER 12

The Bullmastiff Comes to North America

The story of Bullmastiffs in the United States and Canada has been so interwoven from the start that it is almost impossible to separate the history of the breed in one country from its history in the other. We do not know when the first Bullmastiff was brought to North America, but we do know ships from England brought livestock as well as colonists. Surely some early settler brought along his Night Dog or Bull and Mastiff.

EARL HART'S ADVENTURES

The Spring 1963 newsletter of the Bullmastiff Breeders Society of America (formerly the Bullmastiff Breeders Society of North America) quotes a diary entry of an Englishman named Jay M. Laurence. This entry relates the adventures of his friend Earl G. Hart. Hart was Anglo-Irish and lived in County Kildare, where he grew up taking care of horses and dogs. He was a well-traveled young man, making trips to the United States and South Africa in his vocation of horse and dog trainer.

He was at Dorking, England, in 1879, when he met and married Annie. His new wife was the proud owner of a Bullmastiff puppy named Capy, and Hart promptly fell in love with the breed.

An unknown dog, probably from the 1930s or early 1940s.

Bullmastiff on record was born in the United States. The litter consisted of a singleton puppy bitch named Nightheart Princess, who was called Prim.

In 1888 the Harts, accompanied by Prim, left the United States and returned to the family farm in Kildare. Prim was bred three times after the Hart's return and whelped 25 Bullmastiffs. However, it is not known whether any of her many offspring found their way into the pedigrees of the foundation dogs of the breed. Hart continued with Bullmastiffs until his death in 1933. It is interesting to speculate that perhaps the Bullmastiffs later brought to the United States had a Prim descendant in the many unrecorded cross-breeds used in the formation of the breed.

They decided to immigrate to Boston in the late fall of 1880. Hart purchased a yearling Bullmastiff bitch named Bernie to accompany Capy to America. Unfortunately, the passage was rough, Bernie took a fall chasing the ship's cat and, to Hart's dismay, died at sea. Hart's ambition of becoming a Bullmastiff breeder was therefore put on hold until his nephew, Derek, finally brought over a Bullmastiff bitch named Maggie in early 1884.

Capy, although nearly six years old at this point, still knew his stuff, and in December 1884 the first

JOHN CROSS AND THE FIRST SHOW WINNER

Although John W. Cross, Jr., was not the first American to import Bullmastiffs, he may definitely be considered the Father of the Breed in North America. Cross was an influential member of the Westminster Kennel Club, and it was due to his efforts and considerable influence that the American Kennel Club recognized Bullmastiffs for entry into the Stud Book in December 1933. The AKC subsequently adopted the British Bullmastiff League standard, which was the standard in effect in Britain at the time.

The first Bullmastiff registered by the American Kennel Club was the fawn bitch Fascination of Felons Fear (Farcroft Felons Frayeur out of Farcroft Fortitude), bred by Sam Moseley in Britain and owned by Cross. This registration was listed in the AKC Stud Book on March 1, 1934. Fascination, whelped March 18, 1933, was given the registration number 914895. In October 1934 Cross also registered the first Bullmastiff dog, Founder of Felons Fear, also bred by Moseley.

The honor of being the first American-bred Bullmastiff to be registered in the Stud Book goes to the bitch Felons Fear Forest Fawn, whelped January 9, 1935, and bred, of course, by Cross. Her sire was Founder of Felons Fear and her dam was Fascination of Felons Fear.

Through Cross's influence as show chairman of the Westminster Kennel Club, the first classes for Bullmastiffs at a North American dog show were offered at the 1934 Westminster show. Cross had his own Bullmastiff to show, but wanted to be sure other Bullmastiffs would be there, as well. This turned out to be no easy task. He heard about a two-year-old Bullmastiff dog in the Philadelphia area and went about locating the owner. This was a young man named Pat Hagen, and the dog was Fenn's First, purchased from J. V. Toney in Britain. Cross persuaded Hagen to enter his dog at the Westminster show so that Cross's bitch, Fascination of Felons Fear, would have some competition. As so often happens to exhibitors who invite competition, Hagen's dog placed first and Cross's bitch placed second. Fenn's First was never registered with the American Kennel Club, and no further

Am./Eng. Ch. Jeanette of Brooklands of Felons Fear, the first AKC-KC dual champion. She whelped only one litter in the United States, and her bloodline did not continue here. (J. Ingam & Sons)

record has been found of him or Hagen. However, Hagen does have the distinction of owning the first Bullmastiff to win a ribbon at a North American dog show. It would take forty years before a Bullmastiff won Best in Show at an AKC all-breed show.

The Stud Book of March 1, 1936, records the most famous of Cross's imports, Jeanette of Brooklands. Jeanette was a fawn bitch bred by Tom Pennington and sold to Cross by E. L. Spruce of Brooklands Bullmastiffs, a British kennel. She was selected for Cross by the well-known professional handler and later AKC judge Percy Roberts.

She was registered in the Stud Book as Jeanette of Brooklands of Felons Fear. Jeanette easily obtained her AKC Championship. She also became the first Bullmastiff to win the Working Group in the United States.

On May 16, 1937, Jeanette whelped a litter by Farcroft Foreman of Felons Fear. There were two puppies registered from this litter: Mister Mac of Felons Fear and Dinro King. Cross later became ill and ended his involvement in dogs, and Jeanette was returned to Britain. She won her third Challenge Certificate in July 1939, becoming the first AKC–KC dual Champion.

In all, Cross imported two dogs and five bitches, including six Farcroft Bullmastiffs from Moseley's kennel. He registered 21 Bullmastiffs from three of the bitches. Records indicate that only three of these 21 were bred. All three were daughters of Fascination, Cross's first bitch.

Rodenhurst Rajah was three months older than Ruby, and illustrates the type of the day.

However, only one of these three litters was bred by Cross. The line comes to an end with a great-grandson of Fascination named Red Jack of the Country Kitchen, whelped February 1, 1944. His sire was Red Duke of Bedford Hills, a son of Strawberry Hill Frieda (Farcroft Foreman of Felons Fear out of Fascination of Felons Fear).

Although Cross's breeding program did not contribute to the present-day Bullmastiff, the fancy owes him a debt of gratitude for his work in getting the breed recognized and accepted so quickly in North America. We are indeed fortunate that an individual of Cross's stature and influence became interested in the breed.

THE EARLY PIONEERS

The second person to import and register a Bullmastiff was Alice M. Anderson. Her bitch, Chestonian Grand Slam (Tigers Vindictive out of Trixie Girl), was whelped in 1934 and registered in the United States in 1936. The same year she also registered the imported dog Neil (Simba out of Freya of Germains), who was whelped in 1933. She wasted no time in introducing her two imports, and a litter was whelped on July 1, 1936. Three puppies were registered from this litter. She repeated the breeding in 1938, and five puppies were registered.

Neil also sired a litter out of Strawberry Hill Frieda (bred by Cross), and another litter out of Bess of the Fenns (imported by Arthur Ponsonby). None of the puppies out of Bess ever had registered offspring. Anderson's main contribution was in giving the breed exposure by competing in the show ring with Cross's dogs.

She also influenced the breed in another way. Anderson's husband was a partner in J. P. Morgan and Co., which formed the Continental Oil Corporation (Conoco) in 1929. Daniel J. Moran, Conoco's chairman, was the first American breeder to leave his mark on our modern dogs, and no doubt he was introduced to the breed by the Andersons.

Most of Moran's breeding was done on his lovely Mo-Ranch in the hill country of Texas, near Houston. (Mo-Ranch is now mostly a state park, and the house is a Presbyterian convention center.) Moran started by importing Rodenhurst Ruby, a British bitch bred by J. J. Heaton and selected for him by Charles H. Turner. Ruby was red fawn with a black mask. Her sire was Phantom of Crestwood and her dam was Patricia of Crestwood. Ruby became the first foundation bitch of the modern North American Bullmastiff.

Moran's foundation sire was also imported by Turner. This was the dog Bluff, bred by F. H. Robinson and registered in the United States in 1937. This brindle dog's sire was Mackwyn Excelsior and his dam was Woodacre Stormer.

Bluff, bred back to his and Ruby's daughter, Farvale Sentinel, produced the dark brindle dog Pride of Elgin, whelped in 1939 and bred by Edna M. Bowman. Pride was sold to Byron W. Parker of Ontario, and in 1940 became the first Bullmastiff to be registered with the Canadian Kennel Club. Pride of Elgin is in the pedigrees of most Bullmastiff lines in North America today (unless they come from fairly recent British imports).

Altogether there were 14 puppies registered from Bluff out of Ruby breedings. Among the

Eng. Ch. Mackwyn Excelsior, a well-used early stud dog, still showing the Night Dog type.

more noted owners of Mo-Ranch Bullmastiffs were William O. Armstrong, Bradley Goodyear and Arthur A. Andersen. In spite of the fact that Moran bred many litters, Pride of Elgin was the only one of his stock to really have an impact on the modern Bullmastiff.

THE CALIFORNIA CONTINGENT

The next importer to leave his mark on the modern Bullmastiff was Victor Dane of Tarzana, California. He imported the fawn dog Toby of LeTasyll (Fawn Prince out of Tigers Repeater), whelped in 1937 and bred by R. Bullough.

Another of Dane's important imports was the red fawn bitch Fairhazel Jenny (Peter Bighead out of Shy Girl), whelped in 1937 and bred by P. E. Kisby.

The reason Toby and Jenny are so important to North American Bullmastiff history is that in 1940 they produced Harbex Duchess, a red fawn daughter with a black mask. Harbex Duchess was purchased by Byron W. Parker of Ontario and was bred to his other important purchase—Pride of Elgin. Parker's Parkhurst prefix became a lynchpin of many breeding programs, both in Canada and the eastern United States.

It should be noted that the Harbex prefix originated and was still used by Frances Warren in Britain at the time. Victor Dane imported several of her Harbex Bullmastiffs, and whether or not she approved of Dane using her Harbex prefix on dogs that he bred in the United States is not known. Warren wrote of sending several dogs to the United States during the war years to preserve her strain, and it is possible she thought of bringing some of their progeny back to Britain when the war was over. Her Harbex prefix was also used by Parker in Canada on a dog he bred and named Harbex of Parkhurst. The indiscriminate use of the name has made researching these early dogs very difficult.

Dane's energetic breeding program sparked an upsurge in Bullmastiffs on the West Coast in the early and mid-1940s. Harry and Hilda McAfee purchased several of Dane's dogs and initially bred under the kennel prefix Britian's, but later changed their prefix to Harhill. Gertrude Bibo also purchased seed stock from Dane, and used the prefix Elnido for her breeding efforts.

It was during this period that Harry M. Warner purchased Mike, a Bullmastiff whelped in 1941, sired by Monopoly of Harbex out of Fairhazel Jenny. Mike was a great favorite of the movie stars at Warner Brothers Studios, and Douglas Fairbanks, Jr., subsequently bought a puppy for himself. Lita Heller, the daughter of Harry and Lena (Basquette) Warner, still maintains Bullmastiffs as house pets and companions. (Her mother Lena went on to found the noted Honey Hollow Great Dane Kennel, and became a well-known and colorful professional dog handler, author and AKC judge.)

That flurry of activity and popularity had run its course by June 1945, when the last Harhill litter was whelped. The Toby-Jenny bloodline had almost died out in its California birthplace when a last flicker was saved. A bitch, Lady Toni of Harhill, was mated to a British import named Brave Pride in 1949 to produce Leonid. He was owned by Glade Clark and was used by Leonard V. Smith in his early Bullmast breeding program, thus saving the genes for posterity. The McAfees' last contribution to the breed was Big Gun of Bulmas, imported from Britain in 1952.

RICH AS ROCKEFELLER

The John D. Rockefeller, Jr., story is another example of how the wealthy were attracted to the Bullmastiff breed in the early days. Rockefeller had an elegant estate near Tarrytown, New York, called Pocantico. It is not known whether he had a problem with poachers, or was simply introduced to the breed by Cross or others. Regardless of the reason, his gamekeeper, D. M. MacVicar, imported Chang Felius, along with three other dogs and a bitch. All were registered in the AKC Stud Book in 1939. MacVicar later also imported the bitch Dorothy Gay, registered in 1941.

Two of these imported Bullmastiffs influenced our modern dogs, so it is important to look a bit deeper into their pedigrees. Chang Felius (Bedhampton Chang out of Trustful Fawn) was whelped in 1933, bred by A. F. Putnam. Dorothy Gay (Max out of Stall Owners Stormer) was whelped in 1938, bred by Jasper Trodden.

Chang Felius was bred to Dorothy Gay, and the litter was whelped in 1941. Three dogs and three bitches were registered from this litter. Rockefeller kept all except the bitch Taurus Tigress, who was registered to MacVicar. Rockefeller made only a few more Bullmastiff breedings, and those may be ignored because the offspring are not pertinent to the history of the breed. He continued his interest in the breed with the purchases of Cedric of Harhill from the McAfees in 1947 and Timothy Woods Jason from Lois E. Howard in 1952.

MacVicar mated his bitch Taurus Tigress to her brother, Pocantico Permit. The 1943 litter included the bitch Princess Chloe, who became a very important part of Bullmastiff history. Princess Chloe was sold to Stanley Wolff, who bred her to her dam's brother, Pocantico Pathfinder. From this union in 1946, she produced Lancelot of Northcastle (the first recipient of the LeTasyll Cup in 1950 for outstanding dog of the year), Sir Tristan of Northcastle, Princess Thule of Stornoway, Pocantico Robin Hood, Dotson's Own Chloe and

Ch. Lancelot of Northcastle, the first recipient of the LeTasyll Cup.

Pocantico Snowshoe. Lancelot was an inbred dog, described by contemporary breeders as being of the Mastiff type and weighing around 170 pounds.

MacVicar's last major contribution to the breed was the gift of a puppy from the Pathfinder out of Chloe litter to a young lady named Edith Pyle. This present kindled her interest in the breed, and she was to have considerable influence in the years to come.

THE CANADIAN PIONEER

Byron Parker of Ontario, Canada, was another pioneer of the breed in North America. We have already mentioned his two excellent purchases, Pride of Elgin and Harbex Duchess. From these two, he established one of the great breeding programs in his Parkhurst Kennel. He later imported the dog Stanfella of Bablock to add diversity to his breeding.

One of the early great Bullmastiff stud dogs was Ch. Heatherbelle Emperor (Pride of Elgin out of Harbex Duchess), who Parker sold to H. W. and Heather Mellish of Vancouver, British Columbia.

The Mellish's unselfish devotion to dogs must be noted. They kept both Bullmastiffs and Mastiffs. The hardships the people of Britain suffered during World War II severely decimated the Mastiff breed in their home country. The fanciers there were so desperate that dogs suspected to be Bullmastiffs were being used in an attempt to save the Mastiff breed. The Mellishes sent several of their beloved Mastiffs to Britain in order to expand the gene pool sufficiently to make the breed viable again.

They did very good work in breeding Bullmastiffs, as well. They purchased the British bitch Charlotta of LeTasyll, who they bred to Emperor to produce Heatherbelle Lady Margaret. Margaret

was bred back to Emperor to produce Heatherbelle Margaret's Jenny, the bitch Edie Pyle considered to be the foundation of her great line.

D.J. AND THE BULLMASTIFF CLUB

Another individual who was to have great impact on the breed in North America purchased her first Bullmastiff in 1936. Dorothea Daniell-Jenkins bought a grandson of Tiger Taurus from a breeder near Swansea in Wales. She named the puppy Tiger. She and her husband John relocated to Canada, and in 1939 Tiger became a Canadian resident. There were probably Bullmastiffs before that in Canada, but Tiger is the first we could find of which there is a record. The Daniell-Jenkins's did not register Tiger with the Kennel Club before leaving Britain, and unfortunately, when they later attempted to contact his breeder to remedy the situation, they discovered the breeder had moved and could not be traced. Consequently, Tiger was never registered in Britain or Canada. However D.J., as she came to be fondly

---

PARKER'S PRIDE

Some of the other significant Bullmastiffs produced by Byron Parker were:

Pride of Parkhurst II (Stanfella of Bablock out of Lady Eden), who was Edie Pyle's foundation sire
Brewster's Duchess of Parkhurst (Stanfella of Bablock out of Nancy Bell of Parkhurst), who became Twit-Lee Kennel's first great brood bitch
Eden and Lady Eden (Pride of Elgin out of Harbex Duchess)
Heatherbelle Empress (Eden out of Lady Eden)
Lady Roosevelt of Parkhurst (Pride of Elgin out of Harbex Duchess), owned by Gen. Elliott Roosevelt (Franklin Roosevelt's son)

known, would later influence the breed, both as a breeder and through her judging in Canada, Great Britain and the United States.

Her second dog, acquired after the death of Tiger in 1947, was Ch. Robin of the Rouge (Robin Hood of LeTasyll out of Betty of Stanfell), bred by Dorothy J. Nash. Robin was a cornerstone of the breed, both in Canada and the United States.

A bitch was needed, so Daniell-Jenkins bought Rosalind of the Rouge (Rhodian Junior out of Mimico Marionette), bred by Marjorie E. Lawton. The Rouge kennel was then ready to make a name for itself in Bullmastiff history, and became a major influence for many years.

Daniell-Jenkins was a popular judge and was in frequent demand to judge breed specialty shows. In 1950 she was also instrumental in reviving interest in a breed club in the United States. (Robert Lee and Irene Twitty, Lois Aitken, Edith Pyle and James Mossman were also part of the group working for a new club.) The Bullmastiff Club of America had been allowed to lapse in the years after its formation in 1935, and was not recognized by the American Kennel Club. Daniell-Jenkins and the Twittys brought Dorothy J. Nash of the famous LeTasyll Bullmastiff Kennel in Britain to the United States to lecture on the Bullmastiff, in an attempt to arouse interest in a club. Nash brought a pewter Rose Bowl with her, which she donated to the re-formed club. The trophy, which came to be

Eng. Ch. Robin Hood of LeTasyll. His blood, imported to northeastern Canada, was of great influence in early breedings.

TOP IMPORTS

Other important Daniell-Jenkins imports include:

Tasmar Bridget of LeTasyll (Robin Hood of LeTasyll out of Maritime Copyright), bred by G. Mitchley

Tudor Queen of LeTasyll (Tasmar Bandit out of Roberta of LeTasyll), bred by D. L. Bayliss

Robin Hi Ho of Hopperkid (Robin Hood of LeTasyll out of Carrokid Jane), bred by E. Bolton.

named the LeTasyll Cup, was awarded by the board of directors of the club to the most outstanding Bullmastiff each year. The names of the recipients were engraved on silver shields on the ebony base of the trophy. The club was successful, and operated for six years under the name of its predecessor, the Bullmastiff Club of America.

Daniell-Jenkins was also one of the driving forces behind the formation of the national breed club in Canada in 1951. The club was first named the Honourable Company of Bullmastiff Fanciers in Canada. It was later changed to the more modern Bullmastiff Fanciers of Canada. Their first specialty show was held September 15, 1951, in conjunction with the Progressive Kennel Club of Canada, located in Dixie, Ontario. Col. E. D. McQuown was the judge, and 26 dogs were entered. Ch. Robin of the Rouge won Best of Breed, with Ch. Binagain of Bulmas, owned by Robert Lee and Irene Twitty, taking Best of Opposite Sex. McQuown liked Robin and also awarded him first place in the Working Group that day, as well as the first all-breed Best in Show in the Americas.

Daniel-Jenkins exhibited her dogs both in Canada and the eastern United States, and many kennels of the day in both countries had a Rouge Bullmastiff in them.

MORE CANADIAN PIONEERS

Paul Burden was also an early Canadian breeder. He established his Polira Kennel on the successful Mulorna line of Doris Mullins in Britain. He used the bloodlines of Hector of Mulorna, Sylvia of

Am./Can. Ch. Stentor of the Rouge, one of Daniell-Jenkins' favorites.

Mulorna and Pioneer of Mulorna in forming this effective breeding program.

Marjorie E. Lawton established her Majfern Kennel and instituted a successful breeding program. She imported Rhodian Junior, Collier Boy and Mimico Marionette. Foster Law imported Bulletproof of Bulmas and Beautiful Gem of Bulmas. R. Phillips imported another Mulorna bitch, Avril of Mulorna, and the Mellishes purchased Charlotta of LeTasyll. This nucleus of breeders, together with Parker, served as the foundation for the breed in Canada.

Then, as now, there were a great number of dogs moving between Canada and the United States, and this helped the breed at a time when total numbers were very low.

THE NEXT WAVE

The second generation of Bullmastiff fanciers included Walter, Edith and Tom Pyle, who continued Rockefeller's former kennel name, Pocantico, and registered it with the American Kennel Club in 1946. They maintained the name for 44 years, until 1990. The American Kennel Club then retired the name, and it will not be issued again.

Tom Pyle, Edie's father-in-law, was employed as head of security at Pocantico, and Edie also worked at the estate for a time. As we mentioned earlier, it all began when MacVicar the gamekeeper gave Edie Pocantico Snowshoe, a bitch puppy from Pocantico Pathfinder out of Princess Chloe. She bred Snowshoe to the Canadian-bred dog Pride of Parkhurst II, whom she bought from Parker. Later she bought a British-bred bitch, Dutchess Threebooks (bred by A.B. Levesley) that was already in the United States. The famous Pocantico breeding program began with these three Bullmastiffs.

Edie, however, always considered her next purchase, Heatherbelles Margaret's Jenny, to be the true cornerstone of Pocantico Kennel. Jenny was bred by the Mellishes in western Canada, and was sired by Ch. Heatherbelle Emporer out of his daughter, Heatherbelle's Lady Margaret.

Pocantico dogs won four American national specialties: Ch. Pocantico Runkles Treasure won in 1959 and 1961, Ch. Pocantico Runkles King won the honor in l962 and Ch. Pocantico Worrysum Favo d'Mel won in 1972. Ch. Pontico Runkles Treasure was one of the Pyles' favorites. In her obituary, they related how one cold Vermont winter day she tracked an old, blind Sealyham Terrier for more than a mile after its owners had searched unsuccessfully all day.

Another considerable contributor to the breed was Ch. Pocantico Runnymeade Monster. He sired many good dogs, and one of his grandsons, Ch. Pocantico Dunworryin Faro (who was Favo d'Mel's sire), is remembered as one of the all-time great stud dogs for the quality he produced.

Robert Lee and Irene Twitty were very wealthy individuals who did not hesitate to spend that wealth in establishing their Twit-Lee Kennel. It quickly became the preeminent kennel in North America, and was known by Bullmastiff fanciers around the world. They first purchased Brewster's Duchess of Parkhurst from Parker, Majfern Guardian from Marjorie E. Lawton and Sir Galahad of Hilltop Acres from Edie Pyle.

Ch. Pocantico Dunworryin Faro, one of the later Pyle dogs, and certainly one of the best.

Twitty was not satisfied with his progress using dogs from North America, so in July of 1950 he imported his first British dogs from Cyril Leeke, littermates Bepagain of Bulmas (a dog) Binagain of Bulmas (a bitch). This was just the start of many imports in a short time by Twitty and others. Twitty imports include Blue Print of Bulmas, Bombhurst of Bulmas, British Maid of Bulmas, Martin of Marbette, Miking of Marbette, Miniver of Marbette, Broad Oak of Bulmas, Aieda of Buttonoak and Ava of Buttonoak.

But importing dogs was not enough. In 1957, Twitty persuaded Leeke himself to come from Britain to the United States to manage his Twit-Lee Kennel. It was wryly said in England at the time that R. L. Twitty, not being content with importing Bulmas dogs, had to have Mr. Bulmas as well.

Despite the advice of a friend (a story recounted in Chapter 11), Leeke came to the United States with the best remaining dogs from his kennel: Ch. Beauty of Bulmas, Billagain of Bulmas, Bar None of Bulmas, Ch. Bright Gem of Bulmas and Ch. Pridzor's Anton of Buttonoak. Beauty, whelped in 1954, is widely regarded as one of the best bitches the breed has ever seen. She won Best of Breed at the inaugural 1957 American national specialty show, which Cross judged. She was eventually to die in 1960 during surgery while being operated on for an intestinal blockage.

While some present-day British fanciers still believe the breed suffered there from the sudden drain of so many top dogs, the Twit-Lee Kennel ended up with a collection of outstanding animals. A number of dogs were bred, including the great Ch. Twit-Lee's Rajah, but as fate would have it just as the kennel reached its peak, Robert Lee and Irene Twitty divorced and the kennel was dispersed. However, the breed in North America profited immensely from this influx of outstanding dogs. Twitty relocated to San Francisco, and his last official contact with the breed was when he judged the initial Western regional specialty of

Ch. Bepagain of Bulmas (left) and his litter sister, Ch. Binagain of Bulmas— America's gain and Britain's loss.

Ch. Beauty of Bulmas, a LeTasyll Cup winner and one of the best bitches of all time.

the American Bullmastiff Association in 1966. Ironically, the Bullmastiff he put up for Best of Breed, Am./Can. Ch. Blackmist Brutus, owned by Geri Powell of Vancouver, was from one of the few lines in North America that did not contain the blood of the Twit-Lee imports.

The influence of top British dogs was also seen in Ramapo Torne Kennel, owned by James Mossman. Mossman wanted a top-quality bitch from Britain to breed to his dog, and bought Yasmin of Glamview. However, he decided to leave her in Britain to be bred to the top dog of the day, Ch. Ambassador of Buttonoak. She was imported to the United States while in whelp. Some of the dogs from that litter, including Ch. Ambassador's Imperator and Ch. Ambassador's Lancelot, were heavily used in many breeding programs.

Ted and Helen Ritter, owners of Almericus of Buttonoak, another import, must also be

Ch. Twit-Lee's Rajah won the American-Bred Class at Westminster and is generally considered to be the best dog the kennel produced.

remembered, as they were the breeders of Ch. Ritter's Beau, one of the breed's great show dogs.

ANOTHER IMPORT

Another British import was Leonard Smith, originally from near Birmingham, England, in what is called "the black country." The name comes from the heavy layer of coal dust and soot deposited across the countryside by the heavy manufacturing plants. Smith had a crossbred Bullmastiff as a boy

Pocantico Red Lyn (shown with Mrs. Mossman) was the foundation bitch of the Mossman's Ramapo Torne Kennel.

Simon of Kareck, the first of Leonard Smith's imports to establish his Bullmast Kennel.

and gravitated to the purebreds as an adult. He became a close friend of Leeke, who dominated the post-war Bullmastiff scene.

The Smith family immigrated to California after the war and formed the very successful Bullmast Kennel, which is still operated by Pat Smith O'Brien. The first Bullmastiff to finish an AKC Championship in California was from this kennel.

In 1949 Smith imported and registered his first dog, Simon of Kareck, of Bulmas parentage. Simon was followed the same year by the bitch Bigheart of Bulmas, also from Britain. One more British bitch, Ballet of Bulmas, was imported and registered in his daughter Pat's name in 1954.

The first Bullmast litter was whelped in 1950. It was from Simon of Kareck out of Bigheart of

Bulmas. The breeding was notable for producing the dog Broughton of Bullmast. Bigheart was bred again to Leonid and produced Beauty, Bonnie, Brenda, Bromford and Brutus Adam of Bullmast. The third time Bigheart was bred, it was to Broughton. This union prodcued Baskerville, Branch, Brumagem, Buster and Benita, all with the Bullmast suffix; and Blimp, Blondie, Butch II and Bimson. Bigheart's last breeding was to Big Gun of Bulmas; it produced Brittania of Bullmast.

Broughton was also used on Ballet of Bulmas to produce Baron and Barnaby of Bullmast, and on

Brittania of Bullmast, owned by the Linebargers, to produce Bounty of Bullmast. Bonnie was sold to Deane Hayes. Hayes bred her twice to Bimson, producing Darcy, Jolie Blonde, Lars and Musette of Morro. Bonnie was also bred to Ch. Baron of Bullmast and produced Hannibal of Morro and the better-known stud dog, Ch. Jubilee of Morro.

Bounty was sold to the Linebargers and was subsequently also bred to Baron. This produced Bright Gem of Bullmast and Broughton Acres Beau Rough. Bullmast made two more breedings: Bright Gem to Red Bluff of Walbar in 1960 and Bronze Venus of Bullmast to Ch. Lancelot's Tommy Tucker in 1963. Frances Martin's Ballerina of Bull Run was from this latter breeding. These breedings were significant in that Smith's early efforts are reflected in almost every line today.

You may have noticed that all of the dogs from the Bullmast Kennel have names starting with the letter B. In the early 1970s we met Smith, and he told us he used the letter as a tribute to his old friend Cyril Leeke, who used this letter in naming his famous Bulmas dogs.

As has happened so often in Bullmastiff history, just when a kennel is dominating the sport, as Bullmast was in California in the 1950s, disaster struck. Illness prevented Smith from personally continuing his successful program. His daughter Pat and her late husband, the very personable Tom O'Brien, continued the kennel on a smaller scale, which eventually saved the line.

The Bullmast line revived further in 1971 when Helen Taylor Hellrich (Hellmark Kennel) bred her bitch Scyldocga Calamity Jane to Ch. Mister MacGustav, who was Bullmast on the lower half of his pedigree. Leonard and Pat were able to purchase Ch. Bullmast Bayard of Hellmark from that litter to use with their remaining bitches. Bullmast dogs are still strong competitors in the show ring today.

There were other 1960s–era Bullmastiffs that also carried the early Bullmast dogs into our modern breeding programs. Prominent among these were Ch. Jubilee of Morro, the foundation stud used by Francis Martin to found her Bull Run Kennel, and Ch. Sophia of Lorraine, CD, owned by Taun Brooks. Ch. Tauralan Tisa, owned by Brenda Gann Campbell, was sired by MacGustav out of the Tauralan import, Bulstaff Coquette of Edialhouse.

CHAPTER 13

The Inheritors of the Breed

By the 1960s, the breeding and sport of showing Bullmastiffs was ready to enter another phase in North America. There were enough imports to ensure a large enough genetic base for a viable breeding population. The pioneers of the '40s and '50s would see their efforts advanced by the builders of the '60s and '70s, who would carry the quality of the breed to new heights.

In 1966 the AKC registered more Bullmastiff puppies than did the KC. This growth has continued, and there are now more Bullmastiffs in the United States than in any other country. Some of the great kennels will be mentioned in this book, but it's important to remember that not all of the breeders and owners of Bullmastiffs can be listed, or the book would be more than 1,000 pages long! However, we have tried to note most of the major players in the breed in the United States during those two decades.

In the 1960s and '70s, the breed was still regional in type, with East Coast Bullmastiff lines having slight but recognizable differences from the West Coast lines. Still, the two decades saw significant improvement in the overall soundness and structure of the breed and a greater consistency of type. This was reflected in the growing number of Bullmastiffs that placed in the Working Group, and the first American all-breed Best in Show achieved on April 27, 1974, by Ch. Chit's Grandson and his owner-handler Earl Dunn (his photo is in Appendix C).

Dorothea Daniell-Jenkins lost her husband, John, in an automobile accident on December 4, 1959. She continued to breed Bullmastiffs and West Highland White Terriers into the 1960s, until the big dogs became too much for her, and then continued with the Terriers alone. Her breeding efforts in Westies

155

made her almost as well-known in those circles as she was in Bullmastiffs. In 1961 she was able to add an AKC license to judge Bullmastiffs to her previous CKC approval. Other talented fanciers took up the torch.

EAST COAST BREEDERS

John and Sidney (Bunty) Van der Valk (Valkenhof Kennel) of New Jersey did not have a great influence through their breeding efforts, but they imported a dog, Bulstaff Argus of Arancrag (a son of the great Ch. Bulstaff Achilles), from Ruth Short in Britain. Argus went on to win a national specialty and would be used to great effect on the East Coast by Mary Prescott (Scyldocga Kennel) and James Mossman (Ramapo Torne Kennel), among others.

John Van der Valk served for a time as president of the American Bullmastiff Association, and a disagreement in the mid-1960s between him and the editor of the association's newsletter, Francis Greeley, resulted in a most fortuitous event for the breed. Greeley resigned as newsletter editor and started his own breed magazine, *The American Bullmastiff*, which became the most pre-eminent written and pictorial history of the breed and has yet to be surpassed. It contained photo advertisements of the leading dogs of the day, and the Greeleys also solicited articles and photographs from the pioneers of the breed still alive in Britain. Eric Makins, Florence Warren, Harry Colliass, Ruth Short and Lyn Pratt were all contributors. These people wrote vignettes about the careers of the early breeders, such as Sam Moseley, Jack Barnard, Vic Smith and others, for the magazine.

Unfortunately, all the breed information Francis and Hazel Greeley used in their magazine was lost to the breed upon their deaths. The few bound sets of the publication fetch upwards of $1,000 when they become available, which is not very often.

The Greeleys really loved the breed, especially their Ch. Ritter's Bonnie. Bonnie was bred to Ch. Rajah's Lucknow Major of Ric Davis's Dunworrying Kennel, and produced five champions from that litter. Davis went on to become one of the few early Bullmastiff breeder-judges in the United States.

A KENNEL BY ANY OTHER NAME

The Bulstaff Kennel of Britain, from whence Argus came, and the Bullstaff Kennel of Vancouver, British Columbia, were not related. Bulstaff (Britain) was in use first and had built quite a reputation before the adoption of Bullstaff (Canada) as a breeding prefix. The close resemblance of the two prefixes resulted in considerable acrimony between the kennels. This dislike was aggravated as the Canadian name became more prominent with the acquisition of Rodenhurst Monarch and the widespread use of his sons, Sampson of Bullstaff and Am./Can. Ch. Bullstaff's Teddy.

Edie Pyle's Pocantico dogs in Vermont were in great demand in the 1960s. Charles Young was not a breeder, but he campaigned Ch. Pocantico Runkles King with considerable success, including winning the national specialty in 1962. Other Pocantico dogs of note in the '60s were Ch. Pocantico Runkles Treasure and Ch. Pocantico Ramapo Copper, both owned by Pocantico Kennels, and the red dog Ch. Pocantico Ambasador Sentry, owned by Cledith and Pat Hurst (Hurstacres Kennel). Later would come such great dogs as Ch. Pocantico Dunworryin Faro, owned by Ric Davis (Dunworryin Kennel) and Ch. Pocantico Worrysum Favo D'Mel, owned by Harry and Beverly Bryant.

Virgil and Adele Millett of New York became well-known through exhibiting their home-bred Ch. Millett's Arguson Red Titan, known as Kicker, and Ch. Ramapo Torne's Red Steve, a Kicker son bred by James Mossman. Kicker never won a national specialty, but Red Steve would set the record by winning an astounding five national specialty Bests of Breed. Virgil also served as president of the American Bullmastiff Association many times during this period, and Adele served on various committees.

Karl and Mary Prescott (Scyldocga Kennel) of New Jersey also had a major breeding program that influenced the direction of the breed. They bred their Ewetyrne's Lady Cecilia to Ch. Pocantico Runkles King to produce the dog Ch. Scyldocga King Ethelwulf. Ethelwulf was then bred to a Bulmas-Bullmast bitch, Ch. Mi-Buff's Baquet, to produce Scyldocga Lady Elaine.

LONG JOHN'S LINE

Some of Scyldocga Long John Silver's notable offspring are:

Scyldocga Caroline Mathilde and Ch. Scyldocga Bairn McGregor, sold to Russell and Helma Weeks (Nutiket Kennel)

Ch. Scyldocga Yankee Rebel, sold to Harry and Beverly Bryant (Favo de Mel Kennel)

Scyldocga Calamity Jane and Ch. Drummer of Stonehouse, sold to Oscar and Helen Hellrich (Hellmark Kennel)

Ch. Scyldocga Bairn MacTavish and Tailwyndes' Amy of Thors Glen, owned by Adele and Richard Pfenninger

Ch. Scyldocga Long John Silver is behind the Nutiket, Tailwynde, Shatrugo and Bastion Kennels, and many others in the U.S. and Canada.

The stage was then set to produce one of the breed's more significant stud dogs. Mary and Karl bred the fawn Lady Elaine to Van der Valk's red import, Ch. Bulstaff Argus of Arancrag. The litter of eight contained the future champions Scyldocga Mistress Crossley, Scyldocga Ben Gunn and the Bronze ROM Medalist Scyldocga Long John Silver. Long John sired Bullmastiffs that would share in the formation of several major lines in the 1960s.

Karl and Mary also started one of the few early brindle lines in the United States when they imported a bitch, Ch. Bulstaff Brocade. Scyldocga bred a considerable number of litters over the years, and puppies from this kennel were used in many breeding programs. Mary Prescott joined R. Lee Twitty, Dorothea Daniell-Jenkins and Ric Davis as an AKC-licensed judge. She also wrote the first book on the Bullmastiff in North America, *How to Raise and Train a Bullmastiff.*

The Bandog Kennel of New York had an excellent reputation. Louise Sanders and Helene Buzzeo (now Nietsch) produced many fine Bullmastiffs using this prefix. The line was formed by using Bulmas stock from the Fortin's Black Knight

Am./Can. Ch. Rowley of Oldwell at eight months—he completed both Championships before he was a year old. He was one of the first imports of the modern type. Although he was imported by Carl and Jean Rabsey, he is best known as the foundation sire of the Bandog/Banstock Kennels. (Gilbert)

Kennel, bred to the British import Ch. Rowley of Oldwell. Later, they would introduce more Oldwell blood by using the import Sambo of Oldwell. Sambo was a half brother to Jack Shastid's imported dog, Ch. Securus Erebus. These dogs were both brindles sired by Justit of Oldwell. Sambo and Erebus founded two of the four brindle lines in the United States.

Among the outstanding Bullmastiffs produced by Bandog were Ch. Bandogs Hard Hearted Hannah, Ch. Huck's Last Hurrah of Bandog and Ch. Bandog's Crawdaddy Gumbo, a Gold ROM dog. Huck's Last Hurrah won the national specialty in 1978, and Crawdaddy Gumbo won it 1984, 1985 and 1987.

Louise moved to Florida in 1981 when her husband retired, and took the prefix Bandog with her. Helene adopted the prefix Banstock in 1981, and has continued to breed with much success using that appellation. In 1997 Helene was approved by the American Kennel Club to judge Bullmastiffs.

Several important lines have been formed using Bandog as part of their breeding programs. Two

1970s lines are Paul Lipson's Brookhaven Kennel and Mary Frazier's Sherwood Kennel. Paul took his Ch. Brookhaven's Pumpkin Pie, of Bandog background, to one of the better dogs the breed has produced—Ch. Tauralan Ted E. Bear, a West Coast dog. From this breeding, Paul got Ch. Brookhaven's Huggy Bear, CD. Big Red, as Paul called him, was used heavily in forming the line. He was an excellent show dog and won several regional specialties.

Mary Frazier used Bandog breeding with a dash of Midwest bloodlines. Among the many fine dogs she produced was Ch. Sherwood's Friar Tuck, and another of the author's all-time favorites, the very impressive Ch. Sherwood's Berry Impressive.

Sam and Ruth Kates of New York formed the Stonykill Kennel mainly from Pocantico stock used on bitches from several different lines, including Scyldocga. A very distinct type was achieved, noted for their strong, blocky heads, and Stonykill became, for a short time, one of the breed's major kennels. Their top dogs include Ch. Stonykill's Red Devil, a Gold ROM dog, Stonykill's Red Devil Dunnit, a Silver ROM dog, and Ch. Stonykill's Midnight Cowboy, an impressive dark brindle.

The Kates finally sold their prefix and many of their dogs, but the line did not end there. Tom and Roxane LaPaglia (Blazin Kennel) purchased Dunnit as a foundation dog and based their breeding program on him.

Helma and Russell Weeks (Nutiket Kennel) from the Philadelphia area purchased a brindle bitch, Ch. Scyldocga Carolina Matilda, and a fawn dog, Ch. Scyldocga Bairn MacGregor, both sired by Ch. Scyldocga Long John Silver, to begin their

Ch. Sherwood's Berry Impressive went on to become a Silver ROM. (Ashbey)

breeding program in 1967. Russell served on the board of directors of the ABA several times. The Nutiket line, while never heavily bred, produced a number of brindles and became an improved version of the Scyldocga line.

In the 1980s Nutiket Bullmastiffs were used to form the foundation for Pam McClintock's Shatrugo Kennel in Canada and Robert and Lynn Spohr's Bastion Kennel in Oklahoma. Both continue the line. Helma joined the small ranks of Bullmastiff breeder-judges in 1993.

The contribution of Ed Schwartz (Greenbriar Kennel) of Pennsylvania should be noted here. Ed so loved the breed that he wished to do something that would show others this outstanding species of dog. So he lobbied the city of Philadelphia, which is noted for its artistic endeavors, to construct a "pocket park," a small grassy area planted with trees and flowers. Ed and his wife then commissioned the artist Victoria Davilla to sculpt a slightly larger than lifesize statue of a sitting Bullmastiff. The result was cast in bronze at Ed's expense and was placed in the center of the tiny park that faces the Philadelphia Art Museum. It is a favorite place of children, who are often found climbing and sitting on the big, friendly dog in the park.

Harry and Beverly Bryant of Virginia founded their Favo de Mel Kennel on a son of Ch. Pocantico Dunworryin Faro and a red brindle Scyldocga bitch. Ch. Pocantico's Worrysum Favo de Mel and Ch. Scyldocga's Yankee Rebel formed the basis of a line that would produce many

champions and spawn bloodlines of its own, including the Fairview, Stonehenge, Saraca and Kismet Kennels. In addition, Harry and Beverly were two of the driving forces behind the successful founding of the Piedmont Bullmastiff Club of Greater Washington, D.C., the first independent Bullmastiff specialty club.

Richard and Adele Pfenninger of New Jersey started with basically the same bloodlines as did Russell and Helma Weeks. The kennel name Tailwynde was registered in 1973. They owned or produced some very good dogs early on in their career, including Ch. Scyldocga Black Azz Ink, owned by Mary Prescott, and Ch. Tailwynde's

Harry Bryant with Ch. Pocantico's Favo de Mel and Beverly Bryant with Ch. Scyldocga Yankee Rebel, the foundation Bullmastiffs for one of the most influential and prolific kennels of the day. (Ashbey)

Gentleman Barney, owned by Richard Watson. Barney was handled by David Saylor to a national specialty win in 1975 and the second all-breed Best in Show win by a Bullmastiff. Ch. Tailwynde's Rinky d'Ink won a national specialty Best of Breed in 1977.

In the later 1970s, the kennel embarked on an intensive inbreeding program that selected for and produced a unique type. The dogs carried heavy bone and possessed very bully heads that were heavily wrinkled. Tailwynde dogs were sought after in Europe, especially Germany. Many European lines now are heavily Tailwynde.

Adele was an excellent photographer and was highly skilled in photographing and promoting her dogs. She also produced beautiful paintings and drawings of Bullmastiffs, which were in high demand both then and now.

Austin and Carolyn Boleman founded their Seminole Kennel in Florida on the dog Ch. Elation's Hey Jude, CD (bred by Mel Murray of Vermont). He was bred twice to Douglas and Mildred Pickles' San Pedro Kennel bitch, Ch. Phoebe Fen Silver. Seminole Kennel is most noted for Ch. Seminole Lone Warrior, one of the early Best in Show dogs. The kennel was later merged with San Pedro and used the name SemPedro.

Virginia Rowland and her partner, Mary Barbara Walsh, founded another great breeding program in Massachusetts. Virginia's husband, Robert Ginn, named the kennel Blackslate after a nearby slate quarry. Blackslate built an admirable breeding program by combining East Coast lines with West Coast lines. This resulted in two Gold ROM dogs, the famous Ch. Blackslate Boston

Ch. Tailwynde's Gentleman Barney enjoys his Best in Show win in 1975. (Ashbey)

Blackie, widely known as Mister, and his equally famous son Ch. Blackslate Boston Brahmin.

Mister was line-bred on Ch. Tauralan Vic Torious, who had been line-bred on Ch. Todd of Teddersbelle. This resulted in very prepotent stud dogs. Semen and the get from these two dogs have been shipped to many states and also to several foreign breeders.

The author of this book judged the 1992 national specialty, and gave dogs that had Blackslate sires Best of Breed and Winners Dog, as well as several class wins. Many breeders of the '80s and '90s have benefited from using Blackslate dogs to help establish their kennels. Virginia joined the ranks of the breeder-judges in 1993.

Left to right, Ch. Blackslate Boston Blackie, Ch. Blackslate's Max of Holmby and Ch. Bad-Nuff Back in Black, all in the ribbons. (Rubin)

Ladybug, founded by Geraldine Roach, is considered another one of North America's great small kennels. It was founded in 1969 with Ch. Ladybug Becky of Cascade, CD. Becky was sired by the outstanding Ch. Pixie's Imp of Cascade out of Vanguard's Blue Flame (a bitch with Bulmas in her background).

Ch. Ladybug's Staff Sargent, owned by Sam and Marilyn Dollin, won the national specialties in 1980 and 1981, and Ch. Ladybug Lady Caitlin, TD, owned by Ralph and Denise Borton, won in 1989 and 1992.

Caitlin was one of only four bitches to ever win the national specialty and the only bitch to do it twice. Her show record also includes seven

all-breed Bests in Show, four regional specialty wins, two supported entry Bests of Breed, 26 Group firsts, 64 total Group placements and 96 Bests of Breed. Caitlin was owner-handled by Denise to all these wins.

Other notables from the Ladybug line include Ch. Roleki's Sampson of Waterbury, sired by Ch. Ladybug Royal Sinbad and owned by Steve and Shane Davis, who won the national specialty in

Ch. Ladybug Lady Caitlin, TD, won two national specialties and seven Bests in Show. (Clint Carlisle)

1979; and Ch. Mikell's Ranah of Leatherneck, sired by Ch. Ladybug Handsome Sampson, CDX, who won the 1997 national specialty judged by breeder-judge Helma Weeks.

Until the late 1980s the Ladybug line was mostly Cascade with a dash of Stonykill. It was then that Gerry bred the bitch, Ch. Ladybug I.M. Chloe, CD, to Ch. Blackslate Boston Brahmin. This outcrossing produced 12 champions out of 15 puppies, including the first two all-breed Best in Show bitches, Caitlin and Ch. Ladybug SeaStar Gem. It also produced one of the greatest show bitches the breed has seen, Ch. Ladybug I.M. Angelica Rose, co-owned by Gerry and Peggy Graham. She was twice named Top Winning Bullmastiff, and was also the first Bullmastiff bitch to be ranked in the Top Twenty Working Dogs in the United States. Rose's son, Ch. Ladybug Thorn of the Rose, BD, owned by Fred and Candy Welsh and Peggy Graham, would garner the same award of Top Winning Bullmastiff in 1995, and also win the national specialty that year.

Rose's daughter, Ch. Ladybug I'm Rose Barette, also owned by Fred and Candy, won the

The author, Gerry Roach, with the future Ch. Ladybug Becky of Cascade, CD, the first of the Ladybug Bullmastiffs. (Henry Kreuter)

1992 Canadian national specialty and was Best of Opposite Sex at the 1993 ABA national specialty.

The line is continuing in the '90s, in partnership with Jack Shastid's Freehold Kennel. Several other lines have also used the Ladybug dogs to good success. The Bad'Nuff Kennel of John and Karen Dorsch used Ch. Ladybug Bad'Nuff Boris and Ch. Ladybug Bad'Nuff Natasha for a breeding foundation. Karen Tremoulis bought Boris's sister, Ch. Ladybug Lucille D'Erie, to begin her Evergreen Kennel. The Dollins used Ch. Ladybug Staff Sargent as an integral part of their Arborcrest Kennel.

MIDWEST BREEDERS

Cledith and Pat Hurst were pioneers of the breed in the central Midwest and were a major influence in that region. They got their first Bullmastiff, Oreland's Red Rose, in 1957 from Peter Chandor of Oreland Kennel. A trip was then made to the kennels of Nancy Johnson, located about 100 miles north of Alberta, Canada, where they bought Chit Sia Yah Loveable, a dog of Bulmas background.

Ch. Ladybug I.M. Angelica Rose (left) and Ch. Ladybug Thorn of the Rose, mother and son, and two top-ranked Bullmastiffs.

Chit was almost two years old and was ready to begin showing and breeding. He soon became *Ch.* Chit Sia Yah Loveable.

Chit sired a total of 13 litters, a very large number for that era. A son of Chit, Ch. Marine Gunner, owned by Earl and Liz Dunn, won the 1967 national specialty. A grandson, aptly named Ch. Chit's Grandson, also owned by the Dunns, was the first Bullmastiff to win an all-breed Best in Show in the United States (his photo is in Appendix C).

Earl and Joan Davis bred to Chit a number of times in establishing their Sivad line. Other well-known lines in the Midwest that featured Chit or one of his sons were Gene and Lila Edwards of Ironwood Kennel, and Keith and Barbara Austin of Wychwood Kennels, among several others.

In 1962 the Hursts acquired Ch. Pocantico Ambassador Sentry. Sentry was a son of Ch. Ambassador's Imperator, bred to one of Edie Pyle's bitches, Ch. Pocantico Runkles Treasure, who had won the national specialty in 1961. His progeny went to the Ironwood, Sivad and Royalguard Kennels, as well as enriching his own.

Tony Schons (Tamerack Kennel), a major influence among Midwest breeders, was a truck driver. On one of his trips in the early '50s, he saw a dog chained up outside of a gasoline station. He liked the looks of the dog but was told it was too vicious to touch. Tony walked out to where the dog was chained, freed it and took it to his truck. That was Tony's introduction to Bullmastiffs.

He soon learned what breed the dog was, and when his pet died in 1958, he bought a bitch puppy from Mr. and Mrs. Paul B. Holcombe. This was Ch. Lady Fawn (Hambledon Mark Antony out of Lady June of Eldona). Tony fell in love with this bitch and would still extol her virtues to any willing ear 30 years later. When she grew up, he bred her to Ch. Chit Sia Yah Loveable. From this breeding came Ch. Cyclone, Ch. Loveable Lady and Blockbuster Blackie.

Tony then took Loveable Lady to Ric Davis's East Coast dog, Ch. Rajah's Lucknow Major, who

Ch. Pocantico Ambassador Sentry is found in many Midwestern pedigrees.

was of Bulmas, Marbette, and Stanfell breeding (all British). Ch. Tamerack's Little John of Major, the best known from this litter, possessed a tremendous headpiece and helped several kennels with their programs. There were few people in the breed in the Midwest between 1960 and 1990 who did not know Schons and his Tamerack dogs. Tamerack was used in the East Coast Stonehenge Kennel of L. Smith and Linda Kight, the GAL-X-EE Kennel of Ed Forsythe and the Shreve Kennel of Dr. A.J. Shreve.

Joan and Earl Davis acquired their first Bullmastiff, Dark Gem of Sunnyhill, in the late 1950s and would become major breeders. The kennel, which they named Sivad, really came into its own during the '60s. The Davis's were interested in Obedience competition, and so proceeded to put the first Utility Dog title in the breed on their Champion bitch. Dark Gem was bred three times: first to Chit Sia Yah Lovable, then to Ch. Almericus of Buttonoak and finally to Ch. Black Knight's Brigadoon. Sivad also purchased Ch. Black Knight's Cleopatra, who was of British bloodlines, from Sid and Iris Fortin.

Sivad sent dogs to several major kennels, including Sharon (Longoria) Sunberg's Royalguard Kennel, Carol Beans' Tauralan Kennel, Ben Baratto's Waters Edge Kennel and the Wilson-Edward's Bull Brier Kennel.

Ch. Sivad Sparkling Gem, bred to Ch. Todd of Teddersbelle, produced Ch. Les' Star Gem of Bull Brier, long the brood bitch record holder for champion offspring.

Ed Forsythe did not breed a lot of dogs, but quality is not measured by numbers. GAL-X-EE would be the prefix on sound dogs with good toplines. Ed used a combination of Pocantico and Tamerack blood. One of his well-known dogs was Ch. GAL-X-EE'S Star Altair, owned by Shreve.

Bert and Mabel Kreutzer (Cascade Kennel) of Ohio were another influence on the breed. The Kreutzers owned a dog that would be known long after their breeding efforts had ceased. This was the famous Ch. Pixie's Imp of Cascade (known as Igor), co-owned with Glen Everett. Igor's grandsires were two of the greats in Bullmastiff lore: Ch. Ambassador of Buttonoak and Ch. Pridzor's Anton of Buttonoak. His grandams were heavily Bulmas breeding. He had considerable success in the show ring and retired as the all-time top-winning Bullmastiff of his day. He is a Bronze ROM medalist and sired a bitch that would become the foundation bitch for one of the top-winning kennels of all time. That bitch, Ch. Ladybug Becky of Cascade, CD, would start the Ladybug Kennel of Geraldine Roach.

Igor's litter sister, Ch. Comet's Penelope of Cascade, bred to Ch. Pocantico Dunworryin Faro, would produce, for Hilary and Sue Norman, their Group-winning dog, Ch. Cascade Hrothgar of Mead Hall, ROM.

Earl and Liz Dunn are not major breeders, but they have played a major role in the breed. Because they both have busy careers, they did not think they would be able to properly care for litters of puppies. Instead, they decided to make their

Am./Can. Ch. Pixie's Imp of Cascade, ROM, looking regal in the snow. (Bert Kreutzer)

contribution by promoting the breed in the show ring and serving the ABA on the board of directors and in various committees. They also were prominent in the Midwest Bullmastiff Fanciers.

Earl and Liz owned Ch. Marine Gunner, Best of Breed at the 1967 national specialty, and his son Ch. Chit's Grandson, handled by Earl to the breed's first all-breed Best in Show in the United States. Earl and Liz also owned and handled the all-breed Best in Show winners Ch. Trojan's Dusty Warrior, the first brindle Best in Show dog, and Ch. Oaken's Ray of Sunshine. The top-10 winning Bullmastiff list each year usually has a dog Earl and

Liz own and handle. Earl became an AKC judge in 1998.

Gene and Lila Edwards of Indiana started their Ironwood Kennel in the early 1960s. They established their kennel on the major bloodlines available in the Midwest at that time. They also were active in both the national and regional clubs. Their Ch. Chit Cavalier of Hurstacres and his son, Ch. Thor of Ironwood, were well-known contenders in the breed rings of the '60s and '70s. They outcrossed to British bloodlines by using the import Ch. Bullpug Buccaner, a son of the famous Ch. Pitman's Gentleman Jim. Later they introduced the West Coast bloodlines of Royalguard Kennel. A number of very good Bullmastiffs were produced as a result, including the nationally ranked Ch. Ironwood's Einstein.

In the mid-1980s, they decided to broaden their gene pool. First they purchased a line-bred Nutiket bitch from Helma Weeks. Then they purchased Ch. Grabull's CC Waterback O'Mom from Bob Gray. Better known as Whiskey, he was a son of Ch. Shastid's Rummy out of Ch. Mom's Red Necked Mother O'Grabull. They also purchased a bitch, Ch. Ironwood's Bailey Shastid, who was Ironwood on the dam's side. The kennel is well into its third decade and still going strong.

Ben and Sharon Baratto of the Waters Edge Kennel of Minnesota are also still active in the breed, the breeding pen, the show ring and local club affairs. They have had success with their program, including winning a Midwest specialty with Ch. Cover Girl of Waters Edge. In the mid-1970s they purchased two bitches, Shastid's Sweet Georgia Brown (Ch. Todd of Teddersbelle out of Jezebel of Securus) and Ch. Shastid's West Wind

(Ch. Shastid's Blue Chip out of Ch. Shastid's Chelsea Morning). One of West Wind's better-known breedings was to Ch. Tauralan Vic Torious, owned by Carol Beans. From this they got Ch. Lady Kathryn of Waters Edge, found in many Midwest pedigrees, and Ch. Lord Dan Book, who was the sire of six champions out of Ch. Arborcrest a Ray of Sunshine and five champions out of Ch. Oaken's Dazzle of Heritage.

One son of Dan Book and Ray of Sunshine, Ch. Tundra's Pinewood Baron, owned by Pam Kochuba, won the 1989 national specialty Best of Breed from the Veterans Class. Pinewood Baron was widely used and can be found today in many pedigrees. He was noted for passing on his correct structure and outline.

Emil and ElVerna Fahse started their Eshaf breeding program with a bitch from Tamerack. The Fahses attended the Crufts Show in Britain early on in their career and imported several Bullmastiffs. The most influential of these imports was Sambo of Oldwell. Sambo was a short but very typey brindle who became an important sire not only in the Midwest but also in the East. Eshaf is also found in the later West Coast pedigrees of Tauralan, Aamodt and Wild Heart.

James and Mary Beattie of the Cedar Ridge Kennel of Wisconsin did not have a long career in Bullmastiffs, but they made several imports of the Misses Goodhall's Goodstock Bullmastiffs from Britain, which helped diversify the gene pool in the Midwest. You will find their dogs registered using not only the Cedar Ridge prefix, but also as Goodstock and Goodstock CR. The program ceased in the 1980s.

SOUTHWEST BREEDERS

There were no major breeders in the Southwest during the 1960s and '70s. The Bentons had dogs in Albuquerque, New Mexico, in the late '50s but stopped breeding in the early '60s. Barbara Coffman had her BoJac Kennels in Colorado in the '70s, based on the Blackmist-Nightwatch dogs from Canada. However, her program produced very few dogs.

In the late 1970s, Bob Gray of Amarillo, Texas, started a small kennel named Grabull, based on dogs from Shastid's Freehold and Winstonsheir of California. The Grabull Kennel eventually produced Ch. Grabull's Brown I'd Hansum Man, an all-breed Best in Show winner. The kennel has relocated to Oklahoma City, where breeding on a small scale continues in the 1990s.

The Franlo Kennel of Frank Gargallo of Houston, Texas, started its breeding program with Bandog stock from the East. Arcenia Rosegrant of Shamrock, Texas, also started her breeding program in the late 1970s with dogs from Freehold and Tailwynde. Antoine and Emely Majors also laid the foundations for their Elyons prefix in the late '70s in Dallas, Texas.

WEST COAST BREEDERS

The western part of the United States and Canada, at the beginning of the 1960s, may as well have been another country. The revolution in travel, both for people and animals, brought about by the commercial use of jets, had not yet happened. Breeders in California and western Canada felt closer to and interchanged dogs more with each other than with the Midwest and the East Coast breeders.

Leonard Smith and his daughter, Pat O'Brien, dominated the breed in California in the first half of the 1960s. (Their contributions are discussed in Chapter 12.) Walter and Louise Pidgeon were well-known competitors with the Smiths' Bullmast dogs. There were several important breeders of the time who benefited from Smith's breeding program, as well. Glade Clark started her Morro Kennel using Bullmast dogs, as did Francis Brooks Martin with her Bull Run Kennel.

Rose Ryan (Winstonsheir Kennel) bought dogs from Bull Run and inbred them to fix type. She succeeded in fixing a very handsome type, but in the process also fixed small stature. This would plague kennels whose lines contained a Winstonsheir dog for years to come.

The Vancouver, British Columbia, area—along with Seattle, Washington—has long been a hotbed of Bullmastiff activity. The Heatherbelle Kennel of the 1940s was succeeded in the 1950s by the Blackmist Kennel of Geri Powell and the Nightwatch Kennel of Bill Watts. They took the bloodlines of Eastern Canada and blended them with the Rodenhurst bloodlines of the Bullstaff Kennel of Vancouver.

Ch. Todd of Teddersbelle, a dog that would eventually be behind almost all of the Bullmastiff Kennels in North America, was of Blackmist-Nightwatch breeding. Ch. Blackmist Brutus was the winner of the inaugural Western ABA specialty in 1966. In 1982 Ch. Baal of Blackmist also won the Western specialty. But these were kennels that

A brace of Winstonsheir Bullmastiffs—typey but small.

did not just produce one or two winning dogs—they continued producing dogs over the years that were at the top of the lists. Blackmist-Nightwatch had the same impact on the breed in the West that the Pocantico, Scyldocga and Rouge Kennels had in the East.

The breeding programs of Blackmist and Nightwatch were so closely entertwined that most breed historians treat them as one. Geri and Bill even tried marriage for a time, but the strong points of view necessary to develop such breeding programs prevented the long-term success of that relationship. Bill retired in the 1980s and gave the kennel name and his remaining dogs to Don Jeffries, who has continued breeding under the marquee. Geri continued her involvement in the breed at a reduced level, and the author was pleased to award one of her bitches, Ch. Blackmist Black Orchid, Best of Opposite Sex at the 1991 Western Canadian specialty.

Another important Canadian kennel, Black Knight, was run by Mr. and Mrs. Sid Fortin of Alberta. Ch. Bronco Bill of Bulmas was the foundation sire of their kennel, and their efforts would be used in forming the important '60s programs of the Bandog Kennel of Jacquin and Louise Sanders and Helene Buzzeo, and the Sivad Kennel of Earl and Joan Davis in the United States, in addition to several lines in Canada.

Back in the United States, David and Lynn Rosenstock of California had a very successful program with their Regalstock Kennel. A Bulstaff bitch was first imported from Britain, and then they entered into a breeding agreement with the Blackmist-Nightwatch Kennels. From then on, the pedigrees of the three programs were almost identical. Dogs would be sent to Regalstock from Canada to be shown to their AKC Championships, while American dogs would be sent to Blackmist-Nightwatch to be shown to their Canadian Championships. This relationship lasted almost 10 years.

Rollie and Carol Jacobs did not have a long career in dogs, but their Teddersbelle Kennel had a meteoric rise and produced one of the great dogs of the breed. They started by purchasing a dog and a bitch from Regalstock. The dog, Regalstock Dawson, was sharp and was not shown. The bitch, Ch. Teresa of Teddersbelle, won Best of Breed at the 1967 Western specialty.

The Jacobs' bred the two, and the result was Ch. Todd of Teddersbelle, a Silver ROM. Todd won Best of Breed at the Western specialty in 1968 and 1969. His son Ch. Big Sur of Bull Brook won in 1973, and another son, Ch. Baby Clyde, won the same honor in 1974.

Todd was not the only champion produced by this kennel, but he was the most widely used. Among the more well-known kennels using him as a foundation sire were Bull Brier in the Midwest and, in the West, Tauralan, Bull Brook (now Wild Heart) and Shastid's Freehold. Brenda Gann Campbell used Todd on her bitch, Ch. Tauralan Tisa, to found her well-known Brodmere Kennel.

Helen Taylor Hellrich and Oscar Hellrich had a small kennel, which they called Hellmark, in San Bernardino, California. Helen was introduced to the breed on the East Coast, where she purchased Ch. Lancelot's Tommy Tucker (Ch. Ambassador's Lancelot out of Bepagain's Patra Anne, a bitch of Bulmas breeding). She made a fortuitous breeding to Brandy Belle of Athenia, who was a bitch of Bulmas bloodlines. This produced Ch. Mister Mac Gustav, who would, in turn, help save the Bullmast Kennel's breeding program in the early 1970s. Hellmark only bred two or three litters, and is now represented only in a few modern Bullmast bloodlines.

Frances Brooks Martin of Yucca Valley, California, became a Bullmastiff fancier in the early 1960s with dogs based on the Bullmast and Morro Kennels. She adopted the name Bull Run for her kennel, and it became very well-known in Southern California. She purchased Ch. Sophia of Lorraine, CD, a bitch bred by the Neubauers. Sophia was of Bulmas (through Bullmast) and Buttonoak breeding. Bred to Frances' Ch. Jubilee of Morro, Sophia produced Ch. Bull Run's Sir Winston Barnaby and Bull Run's Our Miss Brooks, which Rose Ryan used to found her Winstonsheir line.

Sophia was later sold to Taun Brooks. Taun bred her to Ch. Todd of Teddersbelle. Ch. Big Sur of Bull Brook was the product of this breeding. Big Sur was the dog Carol Beans used on Tauralan Thais with such great success.

Taun Brooks, of Yucca Valley, California, was the daughter of Joseph Brooks and Frances Brooks Martin. She grew to adulthood surrounded by Bullmastiffs and acquired her first, Sophia of Lorraine, from her mother while still in her teens. She showed Sophia to her Championship and later to her Companion Dog title. Taun adopted Bull Brook for her kennel name. Sophia, bred to Ch. Todd of Teddersbelle, produced Ch. Big Sur of Bull Brook, who proved to be an enormous influence on the breed.

Taun had bred three litters, which included Big Sur, Ch. Brom Bones of Bull Brook, Ch. Kane's Ida of Bull Brook and Ch. Bonnie of Bull Brook, when she merged her Bull Brook Kennels in 1972 with Jack Shastid's Freehold Kennel in Riverside, California. The combined effort was very successful, producing many champions in short order. The breeding program consisted of Jack's dogs, which were primarily British and Teddersbelle bloodlines, and Taun's, which were primarily Teddersbelle and Bullmast.

Jack added additional British blood to the kennel with the British imports Ch. Frazier of Kelwall, Ch. Drunbar Hotspur and Ch. Securus Erebus. Erebus started a brindle line in the United States and was awarded Stud Dog of the Year in 1976. Erebus was bred to Jim and Ann Bower's Blue Chip daughter, Ch. Shastid's Chile Pepper, CD, and produced Ch. Shastid's Beefeater Phred, CD, the top-winning Bullmastiff in 1979 and a multiple all-breed Best in Show winner in Canada.

Later, after Taun and Jack separated in 1978, she returned to Yucca Valley and resumed breeding under a new kennel name, Wild Heart Bullmastiffs. Taun bred many winning dogs under the new prefix, including the all-breed Best in Show winner Ch. Wild Heart's Samson. She also bred the Group Winner Ch. Wild Heart's Thunder Too, owned by Dione Shastid. Taun remains active today, and is well-known for her skillful handling in the ring

Jack Shastid, shown with Shastid's Chloe at Excalibur, established one of the continuing brindle lines in North America.

and her success with Bullmastiffs in the whelping box.

Carol and Jim Beans founded Tauralan, one of the great American kennels in Santa Ana, California, in 1967. Tauralan purchased Ch. Bulstaff Brunhilde (Bessie) from Carl Rabsey when he dispersed his kennel following Jean's untimely death. Bessie was a well-bred litter sister to Eng. Ch. Bulstaff Achilles.

Carol later purchased another British bitch, Bulstaff Coquette of Edialhouse. She then established a breeding program using these two bitches, which were bred to Ch. Todd of Teddersbelle and Ch. Mister MacGustav. She later bred those offspring back to Todd and Sivad Sundust to establish a line based on these Bullmastiffs.

Ch. Tauralan Tomboy and Tauralan Thais were two of Carol's early brood bitches that formed the basis for her later breedings. A dash of other lines was added as needed to keep the line from becoming inbred.

Ch. Tauralan Ted E. Bear, Ch. Tauralan Thundercloud and Ch. Tauralan Vic Torious, a

Ch. Bulstaff Brunhilde became the foundation bitch of Tauralan, one of the most influential kennels in the world. (Henry)

Gold ROM dog, are examples of the outstanding dogs from this kennel. Vic was one of the most influential stud dogs of the breed. A brindle son of Vic, Ch. Tauralan Hold That Tiger, was the sire of the multi-titled Ch. Blackslate Boston Blackie.

Tauralan dogs were used as the foundation for many lines, and were also used to increase size and substance in existing lines. One has only to look in the American Bullmastiff Association's ROM book to understand the full extent of this kennel's influence on the development of the breed in the United States. Their breeding program continues in the 1990s.

Clifford Jenkins and his daughter Sharon had a short, productive career in the late '60s in El Cajon, California, with their Granitehills dogs.

They imported a brindle bitch, Bulstaff Miranda, who would found one of the brindle lines in the United States. The Jenkinses used her, plus Teddersbelle and imports from Blackmist-Nightwatch, for their breeding program. Brindles in the Tauralan, Wild Heart and Blackslate lines all have Miranda in their pedigrees.

Bill Walkey started his Shayla Kennels near Vancouver, British Columbia, in the early 1970s with the import Cluny of Kelwall, a daughter of Eng. Ch. Frederick of Kelwall out of Eng. Ch. Bonnie of Kelwall. When she was old enough to breed, Bill brought Cluny to Southern California to be bred to the British import Ch. Securus Erebus, a brindle son of Justit of Oldwell. This was the start of a very influential kennel in British Columbia and the Pacific Northwest.

Eventually Bill took in a partner, Jan Scholl, and many good Bullmastiffs were bred. These include Ch. Shayla's Keeper Alargh Dhu, who won the American Bullmastiff national specialty in 1993 and was a Canadian Best in Show dog. Bill is now primarily concentrating on judging and has judged in Britain and the United States in addition to his native Canada. Jan now continues the kennel name.

Jack Shastid became interested in Bullmastiffs in 1968 and acquired his first, a British import, in January 1969. The bitch, Jezebel of Securus, was bred to Ch. Todd of Teddersbelle. All dogs with Shastid's in the pedigree, with the exception of the most recent British breedings, descend from these two.

Jack acquired Ch. Big Sur of Bull Brook from Taun Brooks in early 1971 and campaigned him to be one of the top-five winning Bullmastiffs that year. The next year, handled by Tom Tobin, Big Sur was the number three Bullmastiff in the country. As we've mentioned, the kennel was merged with Bull Brook in 1972, and subsequent breedings used the prefix Shastid's for the merged kennel.

A transfer to the Chicago area left Jack with just one breeding bitch, Ch. Shastid's Anne of Cromwell (sired by Erebus out of Shastid's California Flyer). This bitch was bred to Ch. Shastid/Beefeater Phred, CD, a son of Erebus out of Ch. Shastid's Chile Pepper, CD. Phred was a multi-Canadian all-breed Best in Show dog and the top-winning Bullmastiff in the United States in 1979. According to Working Group judge Lou Harris, Phred made him realize that "a good Bullmastiff need not be homely." The breeding of Phred and Annie produced Ch. Shastid's Willie Nelson.

Another transfer in 1981 sent the kennel to Texas. Jack then leased the Blue Chip daughter,

Ch. Tauralan Tomboy established the well-known Tauralan type. (Joan Ludwig)

Ch. Shastid's West Wind, from Ben Baratto and purchased a bitch, Shayla's Flaire for Shastid, who was descended from Erebus. Later, Ch. Nightwatch Maxwell Jr. would be acquired from Bill Walkey to broaden the gene pool.

In the early 1990s, the American Kennel Club changed their rules and allowed the registration of offspring from matings done in the United States with imported semen. Jack immediately took advantage of this and made the first allowed import of semen from English Ch. Oldwell Saxon of Bournevalley, a Crufts winner and Dog of the Year. The breeding was made with a homebred bitch, Ol West Annie Oakley Shastid, co-owned with Barbara Brooks Worrell. The bitch carried 13 pups, but poor veterinary care cost eight of this litter. The breeding was repeated the following year and produced 13 live puppies.

A bitch, Ch. Licassa Delightful Lady of Oldwell, was imported in partnership with Geraldine Roach (Ladybug Kennel) in 1994 from the Oldwell Kennel to introduce more British genes into the American gene pool. She was bred by Barry Blunden and Chris Quantrill. Jack became licensed to judge Bullmastiffs in 1985. He judged a regional specialty in Canada in 1991 and the American national specialty in 1992. Subsequently, he became the first American Bullmastiff breeder since John Cross to award Challenge Certificates to Bullmastiffs in the breed's native country. Jack's breeding program continues, in partnership with Geraldine Roach.

THE '80s AND '90s

By the time the 1980s rolled around, the regional differences in type had somewhat disappeared. This was helped

Am./Can. Ch. Shastid/Beefeater Phred, CD, certainly not a homely boy. (Missy Yuhl)

along by the advances in jet service, which made it easier to ship bitches for breeding, and by improvements in the interstate highway system, which made it easier to travel to more shows. Fanciers were able to see what breeders in other areas were doing, as well as dogs that possessed qualities that could strengthen their own lines.

The popularity of the breed was soaring, as more and more people became acquainted with the attributes of the Bullmastiff breed. American Bullmastiff registrations greatly increased in the '80s and '90s (as the chart in Appendix A shows). Sylvester Stallone included his Bullmastiff in the film *Rocky,* and that added a surge of unwanted popularity. Later, many people confused the Dogue De Bordeaux in the film *Turner and Hooch* with the Bullmastiff, causing another surge in inquiries.

There were rarely any Bullmastiffs in need of rescue from pounds or shelters before the 1980s. Now the parent club and concerned fanciers are kept very busy trying to rescue and place Bullmastiffs in need of re-homing. The growing popularity of the breed has also resulted in unwanted breeding by puppy mills. These commercial operations are only interested in how many puppies they can produce. More and more, conscientious breeders are requiring pet-quality puppies to be neutered or are selling them with

AKC Limited Registration papers. There were however, also many dedicated breeders to make their mark in the 1980s.

On the East Coast, some of these top breeders include Tom and Roxanne LaPaglia (Blazin Kennel), Mimi Einstein (AllStar Kennel), Fred and Candy Welch and Peggy Graham (Grawell Kennel), Lisa Lane (Zildjian Kennel), Pam Kochuba (Shady Oak Kennel), Dean and Terry Gaskins Aamodt (Aamodt's Kennel) and Linda Taylor (Olympus Kennel).

In the Midwest, some breeders to watch are Gary Anderson (Tondra Kennel), Jean Robinson (Leatherneck Kennel), Anita Lewis and Angie Reese (Azar Kennel), Alan Kalter and Chris Lezotte (Happylegs Kennel), Dr. John and Susan Crawford (Dox Kennel), Julie, Peggy and Jamie Hayes (Hy-Top Kennel) and Lee and Cindy Waters (Waters Bullmastiffs).

In the Southwest, some top breeders are Vicky Lang (Nitestalker Kennel), Mark Essary and Julie Ahrens (Essex Kennel), and Dr. Robert and Lynn Spohr (Bastion Kennel).

On the West Coast, kennels to watch include Jim and Sheila Polk (Tri-Ivory Kennel), Brenda Gann Campbell (Brodmere Kennel) and Dr. Chris and Karen Campbell (Kingslyn Kennel).

In Canada, some top breeders include Andy and Helene Hansmann (Knatchbull Kennel), Pam McClintock (Shatrugo Kennel), Paul and Verna Adams (Gurkha Kennel), Paul and Lynne Rehsler (Banbury Kennel), Mike and Cheryl Kelter (Blackmoor Kennel) and Ray and Sylvia Lawton (Kinanama Kennel).

(*Jennifer Cullison Thomas*)

CHAPTER 14

The American Bullmastiff Association

Owning a Bullmastiff is, in itself, like joining a club. For those who would like to reach out, meet other fanciers and become involved in Bullmastiff-related activities, there are clubs or organizations happy for the opportunity to get to know you. The American Bullmastiff Association is the AKC parent club for the breed in the United States and is recognized as an AKC member club.

This organization is dedicated to the protection and advancement of the Bullmastiff breed. The ABA is also entrusted with the Bullmastiff standard in the United States. There are five objectives listed in the ABA Constitution. Basically, they ask members to attempt to perfect the qualities of the Bullmastiff; to encourage local clubs; to accept the standard as the true blueprint for the breed; to protect and advance the interests of the breed while encouraging sportsmanship; and to conduct shows and matches.

The ABA also sends out information on the breed, educates judges, writes a breed column in the *AKC Gazette,* sponsors a national ABA rescue program, maintains an ABA Web site on the Internet, sponsors a boutique for breed-related items, keeps records and archives for the breed and the club, prints the Register of Merit and the Club Handbook, and regularly publishes two periodicals for the members.

Conducting shows and matches is an important function of any club. (American Kennel Club)

These are the *Bullmastiff Bulletin,* a magazine that comes out three times a year, and the *ABA Newsletter,* which is sent to members every other month and contains information on the club, Bullmastiff activities and other items of interest to fanciers.

JOIN THE CLUB

Any person may apply for membership by completing an application signed by two sponsors, sending the required fee, and agreeing to abide by the ABA Constitution, the rules of the club and the AKC. There are also other terms of membership listed on the application form.

The ABA does not have a formal Code of Ethics, but relies instead on the terms in the agreement on the Membership Application to ensure that members protect and preserve the breed, and behave in an ethical manner. It specifically bans crossbreeding; selling, consigning or donating dogs for commercial resale, raffles and auctions; and aiding or abetting any of those activities. Additionally, applicants agree to be responsible breeders and owners and to participate in breed rescue when necessary for any Bullmastiffs they breed or sell.

Newcomers to Bullmastiffs are encouraged to join the ABA and their local or regional clubs, or a similar organization in their own country. Appendix F has a list of clubs and organizations.

Membership can be simply a learning experience, or new members can dive in and become more involved by offering skills and talents in some particular area of interest. Rescue always needs people to help identify Bullmastiffs in animal shelters, transport dogs, raise funds, check potential adoption homes and foster dogs that are in need of rehabilitation or medical attention. The Webmaster is always looking for recruits to help keep the Web site up to date, the Archives needs someone to put together a scrapbook each year, the Boutique can use help displaying its wares in distant cities, magazines need articles and specialty shows need lots of help on all sorts of committees.

Other organizations may vary somewhat in their activities, but all share some common goals and need the support of a dedicated and enthused membership united in their love of Bullmastiffs.

IN THE BEGINNING

As we mentioned in Chapter 12, the Bullmastiff Club of America was revived in 1950 by a small group of East Coast fanciers. But as people in other areas of the country became interested in the breed, they came to believe a new club was needed that would be more representative of this wider diversity.

Consequently, in 1956 a group of fanciers met at Peter Chandor's Oreland Farm near Edinburgh, Virginia, to form a new club and to hold the first of the sanctioned matches required in order to be recognized by the American Kennel Club. Among the fanciers who attended were the Barnetts from Louisiana, Al and June D'Agostina from Illinois, the Andrews family from New York, the Padgetts and the Hubbards from Maryland, the Backners from Pennsylvania, Gerald and Jeanette Benton from California, Iris Fortin and Dorothea Daniell-Jenkins from Canada, the Bloods from West Virginia and James Mossman.

Sixteen Bullmastiffs competed in the match show, which was judged by Daniell-Jenkins. Shah of Sandene won Best in Match, with Phillips Duchess going Best of Opposite Sex. A terrific

There is something for everyone to do in a Bullmastiff club. It's a great way to learn more about the breed and meet other fanciers.

thunderstorm caused the match to be judged inside Chandor's barn. Perhaps the thunderstorm was an omen of the meetings to come.

The second meeting and match of the American Bullmastiff Association was held February 10, 1957, in New York, just before the Westminster Kennel Club show. There were only nine Bullmastiffs at this match. Best in Match was awarded by a judge named McNulty (his first name is lost in the mists of time) to Ch. Broad Oak of Bulmas, with Phillips Duchess again winning Best of Opposite Sex.

THE NEW YORK CLAUSE

It is unfortunate that the final organizational meeting before the ABA became an AKC member club was held in New York. The ABA was incorporated in that state, and a requirement that the annual meeting be held within 50 miles of New York City was inserted into the articles of incorporation. Although the AKC required that membership be open to fanciers nationwide in order for the new club to be recognized as the parent club of the breed, this requirement of annual meetings in or near New York City precluded a wide participation by members in the Midwest and on the West Coast.

The established breeders on the East Coast wished to maintain their control over the new club, and much subsequent friction would be generated by this article. Still, membership across the United States continued to grow, with club officers and directors elected by mail. To counteract this growth, in 1961 an attempt was made to change the Constitution to allow only those members present at the annual meeting to vote. This was defeated, and mail balloting continued.

The first national specialty was held on September 8, 1957, in conjunction with the Westchester Kennel Club show in Purchase, New

Protecting and preserving the breed is a top priority for all ABA members. This is Ch. Dandini Prince of Oldwell.

York. John Cross was the judge, and put up Ch. Beauty of Bulmas as Best of Breed and Ch. Twit-Lee's Rajah as Best of Opposite Sex. Because all the annual meetings and national specialties were held on the East Coast, the "national" specialties were actually comprised mainly of Eastern dogs. However, the Midwest and California members were permitted to host regional specialties, which sometimes rivaled the national specialty in numbers of dogs entered.

The Midwest and West Coast fanciers finally combined efforts and had the New York City annual meeting requirement removed. The first truly *national* specialty was held in Toledo, Ohio, in September 1978. It was also the first independent specialty (not held in conjunction with an all-breed show) for the breed and the first annual meeting held outside New York. The specialty and meeting were then placed on a yearly rotation between the East Coast, Midwest and California. This arrangement continued until 1991, when the Southwest was added to the rotation. Another region, the Southeast, has been added to the rotation beginning in 2001.

THE LETASYLL CUP

The American Bullmastiff Association came into possession of the LeTasyll Cup in 1963. (The history of that trophy is detailed in Chapter 12.) It had last been awarded by the Bullmastiff Club of America in 1956. The board of directors voted to make the Cup a permanent trophy awarded to the national specialty winner, who could hold it for one year. Starting in 1957, the names of the Best of Breed specialty winners were engraved on shields affixed on the base, thus joining the dogs earlier awarded the cup by the Bullmastiff Club of America.

Setting the breed standard is one of the most important responsibilities of a national breed club.

Names appear for each year except 1982 and 1996. In the first instance, the ABA's membership was in the midst of a struggle over their leadership that had been building for a number of years. The AKC did not allow the ABA to hold a specialty show until the internal struggle was settled. Peace eventually returned with the elections of September 1982, and the national specialties resumed in 1983.

There was a national specialty held in 1996 in Carlisle, Pennsylvania, judged by James Leeson of Britain. However, the Best of Breed winner was later disqualified by the AKC for being shown in a class for which it was not entered. That turn of events left the second gap in the shields on the LeTasyll Cup.

A NEW STANDARD

The ABA made considerable progress from that low point in 1982, and enough cohesion had returned by 1992 that the Standard Revision Committee, chaired by Geraldine Roach, was able to present an acceptable draft to the membership. It represented the fourth proposed change to the breed standard since 1960.

The first three attempts to change the standard had been defeated by partisan votes, but under the leadership of a unified board of directors and the wide representation of the members serving on the Standard Committee, the membership voted resoundingly for the first revised standard in more than 32 years.

The new standard corrected many problems caused by the wording of the 1960 standard, and also brought it into conformity with the new format required by the American Kennel Club. While not perfect, it was a move forward and satisfied the wishes and mandates of the general membership.

(Gail Painter)

Kennel Club (Britain) and American Kennel Club Registrations

YEAR	KC	AKC	YEAR	KC	AKC
1923	5	–	1929	186	–
1924	14	–	1930	194	–
1925	63	–	1931	220	–
1926	114	–	1932	304	–
1927	138	–	1933	378	–
1928	191	–	1934	517	4

YEAR	KC	AKC	YEAR	KC	AKC
1935	584	8	1962	249	123
1936	704	12	1963	238	159
1937	678	15	1964	276	258
1938	706	9	1965	239	230
1939	461	21	1966	207	287
1940	132	26	1967	251	341
1941	80	19	1968	301	308
1942	112	15	1969	322	439
1943	186	2	1970	338	427
1944	237	9	1971	329	535
1945	415	8	1972	443	558
1946	598	6	1973	402	621
1947	784	12	1974	502	588
1948	903	7	1975	369	682
1949	927	14	1976	235	676
1950	899	22	1977	125	821
1951	801	45	1978	324	826
1952	558	58	1979	377	804
1953	616	43	1980	436	918
1954	501	97	1981	422	908
1955	475	85	1982	394	966
1956	432	93	1983	464	997
1957	363	103	1984	530	1,050
1958	316	111	1985	752	1,109
1959	327	113	1986	817	1,063
1960	299	130	1987	801	1,143
1961	284	160	1988	763	1,172

YEAR	KC	AKC	YEAR	KC	AKC
1989	1,235	1,283	1994	1,574	2,333
1990	1,135	1,454	1995	1,746	2,575
1991	1,064	1,715	1996	2,170	2,849
1992	1,133	2,007	1997	2,357	2,896
1993	1,172	2,169			

Ch. Mister U's Music Man, the 1991 LeTasyll Cup winner. (Borders Photography)

LeTasyll Cup Winners

From 1950 through 1956, LeTasyll Cup winners were designated Bullmastiff of the Year by the board of directors of the Bullmastiff Club of America. Thereafter, the winner of the American Bullmastiff Association national specialty won the cup.

1950	Ch. Lancelot of North Castle
1951	Am./Can. Ch. Robin of the Rouge (Canadian Bred)
1952	Ch. Bepagain of Bulmas (English Bred)
1953	Ch. Rodmar's Lady Margaret (Canadian Bred)
1954	Ch. Twit-Lee's Rajah
1955	Ch. Twit-Lee's Rajah
1956	Ch. Twit-Lee's Rajah
1957	Eng. Ch. Beauty of Bulmas (English Bred)
1958	Ch. Pridzor's Anton of Buttonoak (English Bred)
1959	Ch. Pocantico Runkles Treasure
1960	Ch. Almericus of Buttonoak (English Bred)
1961	Ch. Pocantico Runkles Treasure
1962	Ch. Pocantico Runkles King
1963	Ch. Ritter's Beau
1964	Ch. Bulstaff Argus of Arancrag (English Bred)

Ch. Ladybug Staff Sargent, ROM, two-time Cup winner in 1980 and 1981.
(Alverson)

1965	Ch. Bulstaff Argus of Arancrag (English Bred)
1966	Ch. Scyldocga Prince Alfred
1967	Ch. Marine Gunner
1968	Am./Can. Ch. Ramapo Torne's Red Steve
1969	Am./Can. Ch. Ramapo Torne's Red Steve
1970	Am./Can. Ch. Ramapo Torne's Red Steve
1971	Am./Can. Ch. Ramapo Torne's Red Steve
1972	Ch. Pocantico Worrysum Favo d'Mel
1973	Am./Can. Ch. Ramapo Torne's Red Steve
1974	Ch. Charley Hexam
1975	Ch. Tailwynde's Gentleman Barney
1976	Ch. Stonehenge's Big Bad John
1977	Ch. Tailwynde's Rinky D'Ink
1978	Ch. Huck's Last Hurrah of Bandog
1979	Ch. Roleki's Sampson of Waterbury
1980	Ch. Ladybug Staff Sargent
1981	Ch. Ladybug Staff Sargent
1982	No Winner
1983	Ch. Mister Fips N-N
1984	Ch. Bandog's Crawdaddy Gumbo
1985	Ch. Bandog's Crawdaddy Gumbo
1986	Ch. Sunny Brook's Sweet Sarah
1987	Ch. Bandog's Crawdaddy Gumbo
1988	Am./Can. Ch. Shire's Beau Geste
1989	Ch. Ladybug's Lady Caitlin, TD
1990	Ch. Tundra's Pinewood Baron
1991	Ch. Mr. U's Music Man
1992	Ch. Ladybug's Lady Caitlin, TD
1993	Am./Can. Ch. Shayla's Keeper Alargh Dhu (Canadian Bred)
1994	Ch. Blazin's Panzer
1995	Ch. Ladybug Thorn of the Rose, BD
1996	No Winner
1997	Ch. Mikell Ranah's of Leathernek
1998	Ch. Avonlea Storybook Goodfella

Ch. Chit's Grandson, the first all-breed Best in Show Bullmastiff in the United States. (Earl Graham)

Best in Show Bullmastiffs

THE FIRST 10 AKC BESTS IN SHOW

Ch. Chit's Grandson	May 27, 1974
Ch. Tailwynde's Gentleman Barney	August 29, 1975
Ch. Bulstaff Giles (Eng. Import)	February 20, 1977
Ch. Roleki's Sampson of Waterbury, ROM	October 29, 1977
Ch. Huck's Last Hurrah of Bandog, ROM	September 23, 1978
Ch. Kajun's Canu Rufus of Oakbrook	February 11, 1979
Ch. Seminole Lone Warrior	February 16, 1979
Ch. Ladybug Staff Sargent, ROM	September 21, 1980
Ch. Trojan's Dusty Warrior	October 19, 1980
Ch. Bandog's Crawdaddy Gumbo, ROM	February 14, 1982

Ch. Bandog's Crawdaddy Gumbo's record of 37 Bests in Show has never been seriously challenged by any Bullmastiff anywhere in the world.

AND THE REST OF THE AKC BESTS

Ch. Aamodt's Little Cyrus Noble, ROM
Ch. Allstar's Martin Riggs
Ch. Allstar's Mugsy Malone, ROM
Ch. Avonlea Storybook Goodfella
Ch. Bastion's Celebration Time, ROM
Ch. Blackslate's Boston Brahmin, ROM
Ch. Dox Waters Red Rover Red Rover
Ch. Hill's Leo The Lion
Ch. Ladybug's Lady Caitlin, TD
Ch. Ladybug Seastar Gem
Ch. Ladybug Seastar Rosebud
Ch. Ladybug Thorn of The Rose, BD
Ch. Leatherneck Bit of Happylegs, ROM
Ch. Leatherneck's Grizzley, ROM
Ch. Mr Fips N-N, ROM
Ch. Mr U's Music Man, ROM
Ch. Needles Beau Colorado N-N
Ch. Oaken's Solid Gold, ROM
Ch. Ridgeway's Apollo of Carabee
Ch. Shady Oak Dox Fetching Freida
Ch. Upper Crust's Weekend Warrior
Ch. Wild Hearts Samson

CANADIAN KENNEL CLUB BEST IN SHOW WINNERS

Can. Ch. Albertpride Red Dozer
Can. Ch. Black Mist Bo's Black Orchid
Am./Can. Ch. Bastion's Celebration Time, ROM
Am./Can. Ch. Black Mist Eros
Can. Ch. Black Mist Troy
Am./Can. Ch. Blazin's Hurricane Barkley
Can. Ch. Caesar Augustus of Night Watch
Am./Can. Ch. Fairview's Rockin Robin
Can. Ch. Gurka's Mangus Colorado
Can. Ch. Italia's Sasha Grand Zeus, CD
Can. Ch. Noble Nite's Golden Gurka, CD
Am./Can. Ch. Pixie's Imp of Cascade, ROM
Am./Can. Ch. Robin of the Rouge
Am./Can. Ch. Rowley of Oldwell
Am./Can. Ch. Shady Oak Dox Fetching Freida
Am./Can. Ch. Shastid's Beefeater Phred, CD
Am./Can. Ch. Shatrugo Jonathan Q Higgins
Am./Can. Ch. Shayla's Keeper Alargh Ddu, CD
Am./Can. Ch. Vic Ian Ddu of Gurkha
Am./Can. Ch. Windridge Thief of Hearts
Am./Can. Ch. Bastion's Celebration Time

AKC Utility Dog Bullmastiffs

Ch. Dark Gem of Sunnyhill, UD, ROM
Bedlam's Duchess of Gloucester, UD
Blossom of the Empire, UD
Flashing Gem of the Rouge, UD
Granitehill's Rusty, UD
Lady Travis of Bluegrass, UD

Puckerbrush Time I Get to Phoenix, UD
Ch. Uther Pendragon of Dalstock, UD
Ch. Watch Hill's Evita, UD, ROM
Ch. Shady Oaks Velvet Hammer, UD
Ch. Oakridge's Luke Skywalker, UD

American Bullmastiff Association Register of Merit

The Register or Merit, or ROM, is a means of identifying and honoring the top producing Bullmastiffs in the breed. The Register is divided into Gold, Silver, Bronze and Copper. The system awards medallions at each level based on a point system for Champion offspring produced, with additional points given for offspring attaining performance titles such as Obedience, Tracking and Agility. Those requirements are:

Copper ROM	4–7 Bitches, 6–11 Dogs
Bronze ROM	8–11 Bitches, 12–17 Dogs
Silver ROM	12–15 Bitches, 18–23 Dogs
Gold ROM	16+ Bitches, 24+ Dogs

Non-AKC titles do not count. The following list is complete through March, 1998. Bitches are marked (B) and dogs are marked (D).

GOLD REGISTER OF MERIT

Ch. Bandog's Crawdaddy Gumbo (D)
Ch. Blackslate's Boston Blackie (D)
Ch. Blackslate's Boston Brahmin (D)
Ch. Blackslate's Duke O' Sandcastle (D)
Ch. Cheers Better Up The Ante (B)
Ch. Dox Fast Freddy of Shady Oak (D) **TOP
   SIRE
Ch. Leatherneck's Grizzley (D)
Ch. Mister Fips N-N (D)
Ch. Stonykill Red Devil (D)
Ch. Tauralan Vic Torious (D)
Ch. Tundra's Pinewood Baron (D)

SILVER REGISTER OF MERIT

Ch. Aamodt's Little Cyrus Noble (D)
Ch. Allstar's Mugsy Malone (D)
Ch. Allstar's Terry Thomas (D)
Ch. Bastion Celebration Time (D)
Ch. Blazin's Chantilly Lace (B)
Ch. Cadance Firecracker (B)
Ch. Cascade Hrothegar of Mead Hall (D)
Ch. Dalstock Fancy Fanny (B)
Ch. Fairview's Roxanne By Guv (B)
Ch. J-Mar's High Expectations (D)
Ch. Ladybug Bad'Nuff Boris (D)
Ch. Ladybug IM Chloe, CD (B)
Ch. Ladybug Staff Sargent (D)
Ch. Les'Star Gem of Bull Brier (B)
Ch. Pocantico Dunworryin Faro (D)
Ch. Pocantico Worrysum Favo D'Mel (D)

Ch. Prince Chunky Chocolate (D)
Ch. Rajah's Lucknow Major (D)
Ch. Sherwood's Berry Impressive (D)
Ch. Sojourner Queen of Soul (B)
Stonykill's Red Devil Dunnit (D)
Ch. Todd of Teddersbelle (D)

BRONZE REGISTER OF MERIT

Ch. Aamodt's Apple Blossom (B)
Ch. Arborcrest Raise The Flag (D)
Ch. Bairn's Image of Elsinore (B)
Ch. Bakerstreet's Chief Lestrade (D)
Ch. Bandog's Johnny Bull (D)
Ch. Blackslate's Action Jackson (D)
Ch. Blackslate's darlin Delilah (B)
Ch. Blackslate's Little Town Flirt (B)
Ch. Blazin's Brahma Bull (D)
Ch. Blazin's Reflection Dun'N'Lace (B)
Ch. Blazin's Studz McKenzie (D)
Ch. Brigadier of Bullmast (D)
Ch. Buckshorn Red Sky At Night (B)
Ch. Cadance Ritamylipsofkeypor (B)
Ch. Dox I Potatoe II of Shady Oak (B)
Ch. Favo D'Mels Keruth Gordo (D)
Ch. Favo D'Mels Seminole Forte (D)
Ch. Favo D'Mels Yankee Ruth (B)
Ch. Gads Hill's Dolly Varden II (B)
Ch. Gads Hill's George Sampson (D)
Ch. Happylegs Luke of Hartford (D)
Ch. Honey Bee of Country Corners (B)
Ch. House of Tudor's Holly (B)
Kastle Barb Eric Obsession (D)

Ch. Key Por's Brite Brigade (D)
Ladybug Dornsden Bay Bea (B)
Ch. Ladybug IM Angelica Rose (B)
Leatherneck Christy (B)
Ch. Leatherneck's Paper Tiger (D)
Ch. Lindley's Thunder (D)
Ch. Little Caesar D()
Ch. Lord Dan Books Of Watersedge (D)
Ch. Meghan The Guardsman Punch (B)
Ch. Needles Beau Colorado (D)
Noland Zelda of Tecumseh (B)
Ch. O-My's Onest Doc Ivan (D)
Ch. Oaken's Dazzle of Heritage (B)
Ch. Pixie's Imp Of Cascade (D)
Pocantico Worrysum Gal-x-ee (B)
Ch. Roleki Sampson of Waterbury (D)
Roleki's Tara O'Wyldwyn (B)
Ch. Saraca's Shane of Fairview (D)
Ch. Saraca's Syncopated Motion (B)
Ch. Scylgocga Bairn McGregor (D)
Ch. Scyldocga Bairn McTavish (D)
Ch. Scyldocga Long John Silver (D)
Ch. Scyldocga Yankee Rebel (B)
Ch. Shady Oaks Subtle Sylvia (B)
Ch. Shatrugo's Honky Tonk Angel (B)
Ch. Shatrugo's Jonathan Q Higgins (D)
Ch. Stonykill's Midnight Cowboy (D)
Ch. Stonykill's Naughty Angelina (B)
Ch. Tailwynde's J Paul Get'Em (D)
Ch. Tauralan Hold That Tiger (D)
Ch. Tauralan Ted E Bear (D)
Ch. Tauralan Three Cheers (B)
Ch. Upper Crust Carte Blanche (B)
Ch. Upper Crust Double Delite (B)

Ch. Wild Heart's Samson (D)
Ch. Windy Hill's Hannible (D)
Ch. Windy Hill's Luz of Uppercrust (B)
Ch. Oakridge Prinleia, CD (B)

COPPER REGISTER OF MERIT

Ch. Aamodt's Little Lady Royalle (B)
Ch. Abar's Twiggy Magic of Bandog (B)
Allegiance My Friend Kimmy (B)
Allstar's Blossom Dearie (B)
Ch. Allstar's Divine Ms M (B)
Ch. Allstar's hot honey harlow (B)
Ch. Allstar's Mae West (B)
Allstar's Pal Joey (D)
Ch. Ambassodor's Imperator (D)
Ch. Arborcrest A Ray of Sunshine (B)
Ch. Arborcrest Curtain Call (B)
Ch. Arborcrest State of The Art (B)
Ch. Arborcrest Touch Not The Cat (B)
Ch. Arborcrest Woful Countnance N-N (B)
Ch. Arrowhead's Warrior (D)
Ch. Baal of Blackmist (D)
Ch. Bad'Nuff Clamity Jane (B)
Bakerstreet Stolen Jewel (B)
Ch. Bandog's Barrelhouse Baby (B)
Ch. Bandog's Big Time Jake (D)
Ch. Bandog's Devils Delight (B)
Bandog's Jam Session (B)
Ch. Bandog's Maid in America (B)
Ch. Bandog's Midnight Special (D)
Bandog's Quincy's Question (D)

Ch. Bandog's Ragtime Block Buster (D)
Bandog's Sour Grapes (B)
Ch. Bandog's Sultry Sassy (B)
Ch. Bandog's Sybil of Tantalon (B)
Bandog's Tattooed bride (B)
Banstock Shady Oak Happylegs (B)
Ch. Banstock Smart Alex (D)
Barb'Eric's Flash Dancer (B)
Barb'Eric's Major Deficit (D)
Ch. Barb'Eric's Peaches N Cream (B)
Ch. Bastion's Canadian Myst, CD (B)
Ch. Bastion's Fool For Your Love (B)
Ch. Bastion's Lady Love, CD (B)
Bastion CC Brndl Valentine (B)
Ch. Beau's destiny of Rockwood (B)
Bebee of Teddersbelle (B)
Ch. Beck's Wee Wendy of Artuk, CD (B)
Ch. Bedevere of Bullmast (D)
Ch. Big Sur of bull Brook (D)
Ch. Black Knight's Caveat (D)
Ch. Blackslate's Big Daddy Henry (D)
Blackslate's Chimney Sweep (B)
Ch. Blackslate's Diditagain (B)
Ch. Blackslate's Golden Brandy (B)
Ch. Blackslate's Masked marvel (B)
Ch. Blackslate's Moth (B)
Blackslate's Tauralan Tobit (B)
Ch. Blackslate's Whats Up Dox (B)
Ch. Blakes Beauty of Bullmast (B)
Ch. Blazin's Doris Day (B)
Ch. Blazin's Irish Mist (B)
Ch. Blazin's Kublai Kahn (D)
Ch. Blazin's Ninja Warrior (D)
Ch. Blazin's Valhalla, CD (D)

Bluegrass Bad To The Bone, CD (B)
Ch. Bochar's Magic Wand, CD (B)
Ch. Boldwind's Shayla (B)
Ch. Briart's Solar Power (D)
Brodmere's Katiah, CD (B)
Ch. Brodmere's Late Again Sandman (D)
Ch. Brodmere's Ms Sweet Tooth (B)
Ch. Brodmere's Noteworthy Gambit, CD (D)
Ch. Brookhaven's Huggy Bear, CD (D)
Ch. Buckshorn Gale Force Winds (B)
Ch. Bullberry Blackslate Gene (D)
Ch. Bullmast Bayard of Hellmark (D)
Ch. Bullruns Buffalo Gal (B)
Bullruns Sweet Victory (B)
Ch. Bullstar Blackslate Hecuba (B)
Ch. Bulstaff Argus of Arancrag (D)
Ch. Bulstaff Giles (D)
Bulwuker's Destiny (B)
Burnham Mona Me (B)
Catherwood Blackslate O'Eloc (B)
Ch. Charley Hexam (D)
Chata of Organug (B)
Ch. Chit Contender of Hurstacres (B)
Ch. Chit Sia Yah Lovable (D)
Ch. Chit Son of Hurstacres (D)
Colonial's Greta (B)
Ch. Countrylife Crown Royal (B)
Ch. Cresci's Miss Mafia (B)
Ch. Crystal Gem of Saracas (B)
Ch. Cybele of Stonewall Farms (B)
Danchelsea's Fawn Kate (B)
Ch. Danrhonglyn's Grand Greta (B)
Ch. Dappled in Shades N-N (B)
Ch. Dark Gem of SunnyHill, UD (B)

Ch. Darsun's Bede (D)
Ch. Diamondwillow Satin Destiny (B)
Ch. Dox Delta At Dawn (B)
Ch. Dox Shatrugo Lancaster (D)
Ch. Elation's Hey Jude, CD (D)
Esprit Joie De Vivre (B)
Ch. Evangeline's Ivy O'Cresta (B)
Ch. Evangeline's Spike (D)
Ch. Fairview's Little Miss Marker (B)
Ch. Favo D'Mels Faruth Tocado (D)
Favo D'Mels Narcoosie (B)
Ch. Favo D'Mels Yankee Saracas Preta (B)
Ch. Favo D'Mels Sago Sombra (B)
Ch. Gal-x-ee's Star Altair (D)
Ch. Gem's Jorette of Hurstacres (B)
Ch. Georges Royal Duke (D)
Ch. Geste & Billy's Lady Maggie (B)
Ch. Ginger Snap of Waters Edge (B)
Ch. Grabull's Parting Shot (B)
Happylegs Bathsheba (B)
Ch. Happylegs Jeep's Cherokee (B)
Ch. Happylegs Jeep's Sahara (B)
Ch. Happylegs Kinloch's Miss Dot (B)
Ch. Happylegs Levi's Genes (B)
Ch. Happylegs Misty Blue (B)
Hobart Mordred of Druid Acres (D)
Ch. Huck's Last Hurrah of Bandog (D)
Hyhold Third Time Charm (B)
Ch. Ilans Fancy Free (B)
Ch. Ilans Hey Bud (D)
Ch. Ilans Mi-Ami Sunshine (B)
Ch. Ilans Reg Trademark (D)
Ch. Irongate's California Raisin (B)
Ch. Irongate's Chantilly Lace (B)

Ch. Irongate's Frosty Shadow (B)
Ch. Ironwoods Bailey Shastid (B)
Ch. Ironwoods Einstein (D)
Ch. J-Mar Anna Nother Winner (B)
Jagofpeeko Wood Betony (B)
Jezebel of Securus (B)
Ch. Jubilee Arrow of Gold (D)
Ch. Jubilee Governor (D)
Ch. Jubilee Willie Dynamite, CD (D)
Keeper's Countess Christa (B)
Key Por's Lady Luck (B)
Ch. Keytu's Tegar's Rontu (D)
Kimblewick's Banner of Bandog (B)
Ch. Kimblewick's Big Berths (B)
Ch. King Alfred of Sandarr (D)
Ch. Lady Kathryn of Waters Edge (B)
Lady Marmaduke of Arlington (B)
Lady Shennigan (B)
Ch. Lady Victoria of Asgard, CD (B)
Ch. Ladybug Bad'Nuff Natasha (B)
Ch. Ladybug Becky of Cascade, CD (B)
Ch. Ladybug Charlotte Wyn (B)
Ch. Ladybug Ginger Snaps (B)
Ch. Ladybug IM Rose Barette (B)
Ch. Ladybug Mary's Ayla (B)
Ladybug Moonshine Lily (B)
Ch. Ladybug Patchen Hill Polly (B)
Ch. Ladybug The Bishop (D)
Ch. Ladybug Tipperary Red Rustler (D)
Larhaven Ladybug Maully (B)
Ch. Larlin's Scandalous Bruno (D)
Layne's Pandora of Jubilee (B)
Ch. Leathernecks Dream Girl (B)
Ch. Leathernecks Gift of Gab (B)

(American Kennel Club)

Lombardy Estella (B)
Ch. Lost Run's Penny Banstock (B)
Ch. Magician of Bandog (D)
Ch. Mardic Nactarsh of Waystead (B)
Ch. Megan Deines O' Hilltop (B)
Ch. Melkev's Prettywoman Vonhelken (B)
Ch. Melkev's Steppin Out (B)
Ch. Miss Fenn of Woodhaven, CD (B)
Ch. Miss Jug of Pohick Creek (B)
Ch. Moorland's Peggoty of Fips (B)
Ch. Mr U's Music Man (D)
Nanzi of Bandog (B)
Night Stalker Megan (B)
Ch. Night Watch Maxwell Jr (D)
Ch. Noland Erie Forger Jennifer (B)
Ch. Nutiket Shatrugo Cover Girl (B)
Ch. Oakens Solid Gold (D)
Ol' West Annie Oakley Shastid (B)
Ch. Oldwell Saxon of Bournevalley (D)
Ch. Ozona's Magor Missabib (B)
Ch. Phoebe Fen Silver (B)
Ch. Pieface's Spectacular Bid (D)
Ch. Pixie's Guinivere of Cascade (B)
Plandom's Fleur Dubos (B)
Ch. Pocantico Ambassador Sentry (D)
Ch. Pocantico Plameses Bruno (D)
Ch. Pocantico Ramapo Copper (B)
Ch. Pocantico Runkles Treasure (B)
Pocantico Twitty's Arietis (B)
Ch. Polar Teak of Kismet (B)
Ch. Praetorian Believe It Or Not (B)
Ramp Creek Ebony of Ironwood (B)
Ch. Red Sky At Night N-N (D)
Ch. Ritter's Bonnie (B)

Rodenberg's Evergreen Deja Vu (B)
Ch. Rodenbrg's Stormy Weather (B)
Royalguard Desert Flower (B)
Rusk's Honeybear (B)
Ch. Saguaro Domino (D)
Sambo Of Oldwell (D)
Sandcastle Andalusian Bits (B)
Ch. Sandcastle's Bubba O' Middlemarch (D)
Ch. Sandcastle's Carmel Cagney (B)
Ch. Sandcastle's Classy Tasy (B)
Ch. Sandcastle's Hunky Dory (B)
Sandcastle's Liza Ledbottom (B)
Sandcastle's Miss Demeanor (B)
Saracas Deusa Favo D'Mel (B)
Saracas Emerald (B)
Ch. Saracas Sangria Kevina (B)
Scylgocga Bullmast Bronwyn (B)
Scyldocga Carolina Mathilde (B)
Ch. Securus Erebus (D)
Ch. Sedentary's Chevy Chase (D)
Ch. Sedentary's Devilish D'Lite (D)
Ch. Shady Oaks Dox Heavenly Helen (B)
Ch. Shady Oaks Endearing Elsa (B)
Ch. Shady Oaks Great Grr-Annie, CD (B)
Ch. Shastid's CB Protest (B)
Ch. Shastid's Chelsea Morning (B)
Ch. Sherwood Friar Tuck (D)
Ch. Sivad Sparkling Gem (B)
Ch. Solstice Captain Nemo (D)
Ch. Sophia of Lorraine, CD (B)
Stonykill's Black Magic Mam (B)
Ch. Stonykill's Brindle Bairn (D)
Ch. Stonykill's Forever Amber (B)
Ch. Stonykill's Prophet (D)

Ch. Sugaree Roscoe T (D)
Ch. Tailwynde's Amazing Grace (B)
Tailwynde's Amy of Thor's Glen (B)
Ch. Tailwynde's Bump in the Night (B)
Tailwynde's Cat Three B (D)
Ch. Tailwynde's Double Dutch (D)
Ch. Tailwynde's Gentleman Barney (D)
Ch. Tailwynde's Hot To Trot (D)
Ch. Tailwynde's Johnny Walker Red (D)
Ch. Tailwynde's Nematognathi (D)
Tailwynde's Paine Weber (D)
Ch. Tailwynde's Sugar Ray (D)
Tailywnde's Tina Turner (B)
Ch. Tamerack's Little John of Major (D)
Ch. Tantalon's Daisy Mae, CD (B)
Ch. Tauralan Bullmast Tory Belle (B)
Ch. Tauralan Midas Touch (D)
Tauralan Paula Tiger Paws (B)
Ch. Tauralan Shana Tova (B)
Ch. Tauralan Talk of the Town (B)
Ch. Tauralan Tara Ann (B)
Ch. Tauralan Tee Soo (B)
Tauralan Thais (B)

Tauralan Tirra Lirra (B)
Ch. Tauralan Top Brass, CD (D)
Tauralan Trick Or Treat (B)
Ch. Tauralan Triga De Aztecha (B)
Ch. Thor of Ironwood (D)
Ch. Tondra's Luther of Watersedge (D)
Ch. Tri Ivory Bacardi (D)
Ch. Tri Ivory Red Rodent, CD (D)
Ch. Tri Ivory Tuaca (B)
Ch. Tundra's Anne of Watersedge (B)
Vanguard Comet of Anton (B)
Watch Hill's Boudicea (B)
Ch. Watch Hill's Evita UD (B)
Ch. Wedgewood Tizzy Lish (B)
Ch. Whiskey Hill's Bootlegger (D)
Ch. Wild Heart's Iron Eagle (D)
Windy Hill's Loa (B)
Wingard's Bonnie lass (B)
Winstonsheir's Barbarella (B)
Ch. Winstonsheir's Belsameer (B)
Ch. Winstonsheir's Brunhilda Belle (B)
Ch. Zaccheus Maximus (D)
Ch. Zorba of Bandog II (D))

Ch. Dixon of the Green, the first Bullmastiff to win multiple Bests in Show in England.

Bullmastiff Clubs

NATIONAL KENNEL CLUBS

American Kennel Club
5580 Centerview Dr.
Raleigh, NC 27606-3390
(919) 233-9767
http://www.akc.org

The Kennel Club
1-5 Clarges St.
Picadilly, London
W1Y 8AB
(0171) 493-6651
United Kingdom
http://www.the-kennel-club.org.uk

Canadian Kennel Club
Commerce Park
89 Skyway Ave., Suite 100
Etobicoke, Ontario
M9W 6R4
Canada
(416) 675-5511

AMERICAN BULLMASTIFF CLUBS
The National Parent Club

The American Bullmastiff Association
Secretary, Linda Silva
15 Woodland Lane
Smithtown, NY 11787
http://www.akc.org/clubs/aba/welcome.html

Regional Clubs

Bullmastiffs of Northern California
Secretary, Linda Occhipinti
18200 Sycamore Ave.
Patterson, CA 95363

Bullmastiffs of San Diego County
Secretary, Stephanie Carnegie
3875 Cameo Dr.
Oceanside, CA 92056

California Bullmastiff Fanciers
Secretary, Gail Parker
33388 Millpond Dr.
Wildomar, CA 92595

Midwest Bullmastiff Fanciers
Secretary, Lynn Angelos
2617 Gideon Ave.
Zion, IL 60099

Heart of America Bullmastiff Fanciers
Secretary, Izetta Wright
215 St. and 69 Hwy.
Bucyrus, KS 66013

New England Bullmastiff Association
Secretary, Lisa Heffner
90 Appleton Circle
Fitchburg, MA 01420

Greater New York Bullmastiff Fanciers
Secretary, Nicole Ziomek
10 Vega Dr.
Shoreham, NY 11786

Glass City Bullmastiff Fanciers
Secretary, Zoe Murphy
7326 Starlight Rd.
Perrysburg, OH 43551-4669

Southwest Bullmastiff Club
Secretary, Linda Walton
RR#1 Box 174
Indiahoma, OK 73552

Delaware Valley Bullmastiff Club
Secretary, Bodil Aczel
1380 Masi Rd.
Quakertown, PA 18951-5221

Southeastern Bullmastiff Association
Secretary, Alyce Weaver
820 Coffee Rd.
Petersburg, TN 37144

Cascade Bullmastiff Fanciers
Secretary, Susan Christopher
2751 Christopher Rd.
Bremerton, WA 98312

Northwest Bullmastiff Society
Secretary, Pat Pearson
11204 229th St. East
Graham, WA 98338

Piedmont Bullmastiff Club of Greater Washington D.C.
Secretary, Mai Conaway
112 Hawthorne Rd.
Baltimore, MD 21210

BULLMASTIFF CLUBS AROUND THE WORLD

Australia

Bullmastiff Club of New South Wales
Nellie Abela
P.O. Box 89
Bargo 2574, New South Wales
Australia

Bullmastiff Club of South Australia
Kath Marion
Lot J Miles Rd.
One Tree Hill
5114 South Australia
Australia

Bullmastiff Club of Western Australia
Cheryl Gilmore
P.O. Box 398
Armadale
6112 Western Australia
Australia

Bullmastiff Club of Victoria
Rhonda Von Blommestein
P.O. Box 13
Doreen 3754, Victoria
Australia

Queensland Bullmastiff Club
Denise McDougall
P.O. Box 5089
Daisy Hill 4127, Queensland
Australia

Northern Queensland Bullmastiff Club
Casslea Faint
14 Diamontina St.
Wulgurue 4811, Queensland
Australia

Belgium

Belgium Bullmastiff Club
President Jean Loeckx
Waarloosveld 42a
B-2550 Waarloos
Belgium

Canada

Bullmastiff Fanciers of Canada
Secretary, Sylvia Lawton
17318 24th Ave.
White Rock, British Columbia
Canada, V4B 5E7

France

**Club Français du Bullmastiff et
  Mastiff (CFBM)**
35 Av des Pres vendome
78450 Villepreux
France

Germany

Club fur Molosser e.V.
Kampstr 20
45701 Herten
Germany

Italy

Club Italiano del Molosso
Furia Pier Angelo
Via Cerreto No 7
CAP 43035
Felino-Parma
Italy

Netherlands

**Nederlandse Multiraciale
  Molosser Club**
Notweg 10
1692 EM Hauwert
Netherlands

New Zealand

Dominion Bullmastiff Club
The Secretary
P.O. Box 2078
Palmerston North
New Zealand

South Africa

Bullmastiff Club of South Africa
Nadia Coen
P.O. Box 4885
Randburg, 2125
South Africa

Switzerland

Bullmastiff Club Switzerland
87 rue de Montangy
Ch-1775 Grandsivaz
Switzerland

Ch. I'm the Best de Orchis d'Orabel, a Spanish Champion

United Kingdom

The British Bullmastiff League
Secretary, Derek Higginson
32 Beverston
Tipton, West Midlands
DY4 0DF, U.K.

The Bullmastiff Association
Secretary, Mrs. M. Rostron
11 Nicholas Rd.
Chorlton-Cum-Hardy, Manchester
M21 9LG, U.K.

The Northern Bullmastiff Club
Secretary, Mrs. D. Massey
37 Low Moor Lane
Wooley, Wakefield, West Yorkshire
WF4 2LJ, U.K.

The Southern Bullmastiff Society
Barry Blunden
"Evesdrop," Epping Road
Broadley Common, Nazeing
EN9 2DH, U.K.

The Welsh and West of England Bullmastiff Society
Secretary, Douglas Oliff
Wyaston, Woodside, Woolaston
Lydney, Gloucestershire
GL15 6PA, U.K.

Bullmastiff Society of Scotland
Secretary, Robert Taylor
3 Moorfoot Path
Park Court Paisley, Scotland
PA2 8AU, U.K.

APPENDIX G

Resources

BOOKS ABOUT BULLMASTIFFS

ABA Register of Merit Book, Lynn Spohr, Editor, American Bullmastiff Association, 1998.

The Bullmastiff, Clifford L. B. Hubbard.

The Bullmastiff, Eric Makins. (Rare)

The Bullmastiff, A Breeder's Guide, Vol. I, David Hancock.

The Bullmastiff As I Know It, Arthur Craven, FZS, 1937. (Rare)

The Bullmastiff Fancier's Manual, Bill Walkey.

Bullmastiffs Today, Lyn Pratt. Howell Book House, 1996.

Everyone's Guide to the Bullmastiff, Carol Beans.

Guard Dogs, J. Watson McInnes. (Rare)

How to Raise and Train a Bullmastiff, Mary Prescott. TFH, 1989.

The Mastiff and Bullmastiff Handbook, Douglas B. Oliff. Howell Book House, 1988.

GENERAL-INTEREST BOOKS

The Complete Dog Book, 19th Edition, Revised, The American Kennel Club. Howell Book House, 1998.

How to Raise a Puppy You Can Live With, Clarice Rutherford and David Neil. Apline Publications, 1992.

The Howell Book of Puppy Raising, Charlotte Schwartz. Howell Book House, 1987.

The New Dog Steps, Rachel Page Elliot. Howell Book House, 1983.

Second Hand Dog, Carol Benjamin. Howell Book House, 1988.

ADDITIONAL READING

The American Bullmastiff
A magazine published by Hazel and Francis Greeley from 1967 to 1979.

American Bullmastiff Association Archives
A pedigree/photo magazine published by the ABA from 1991 to 1996.

The Bulletin
The official journal of the American Bullmastiff Association.

The Bullmastiff Annual
A yearly publication by Hoflin Publications Ltd. It has been published since 1993.

The Bullseye
A magazine published by Carol Beans.

The Pedigree Pictorial
An annual magazine published by Carol Beans.

Index